SURREALIST LEE MILLER

By Antony Penrose

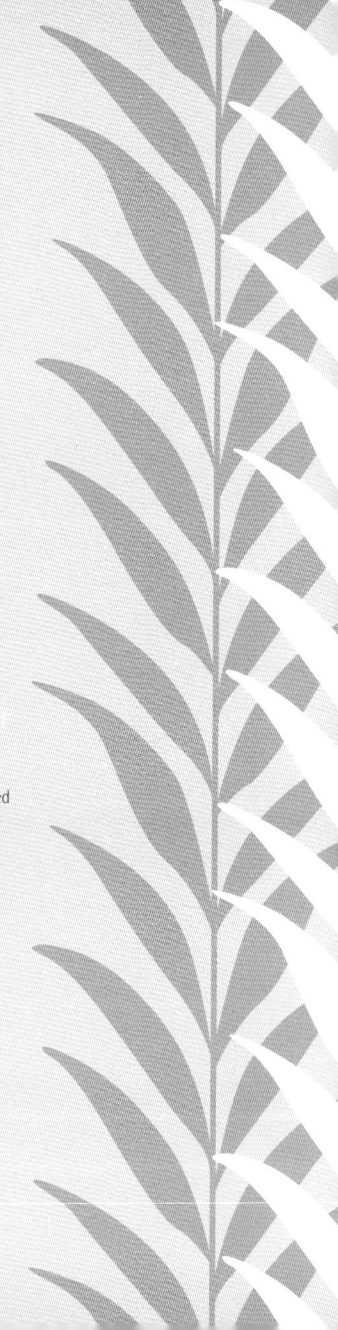

FIRST EDITION: Lee Miller Archives 1998
REVISED AND EXTENDED EDITION: © Lee Miller Archives

Farleys House and Gallery are the managing agents of the Lee Miller Archives
Farleys House, Muddles Green, East Sussex, BN8 6HW, England
www.leemiller.co.uk

A catalogue record of this book is available from the British Library.

ISBN 978 0 9532389 3 4

Designed by FOURLY and the Lee Miller Archives.

Printed in the UK by FOURLY.

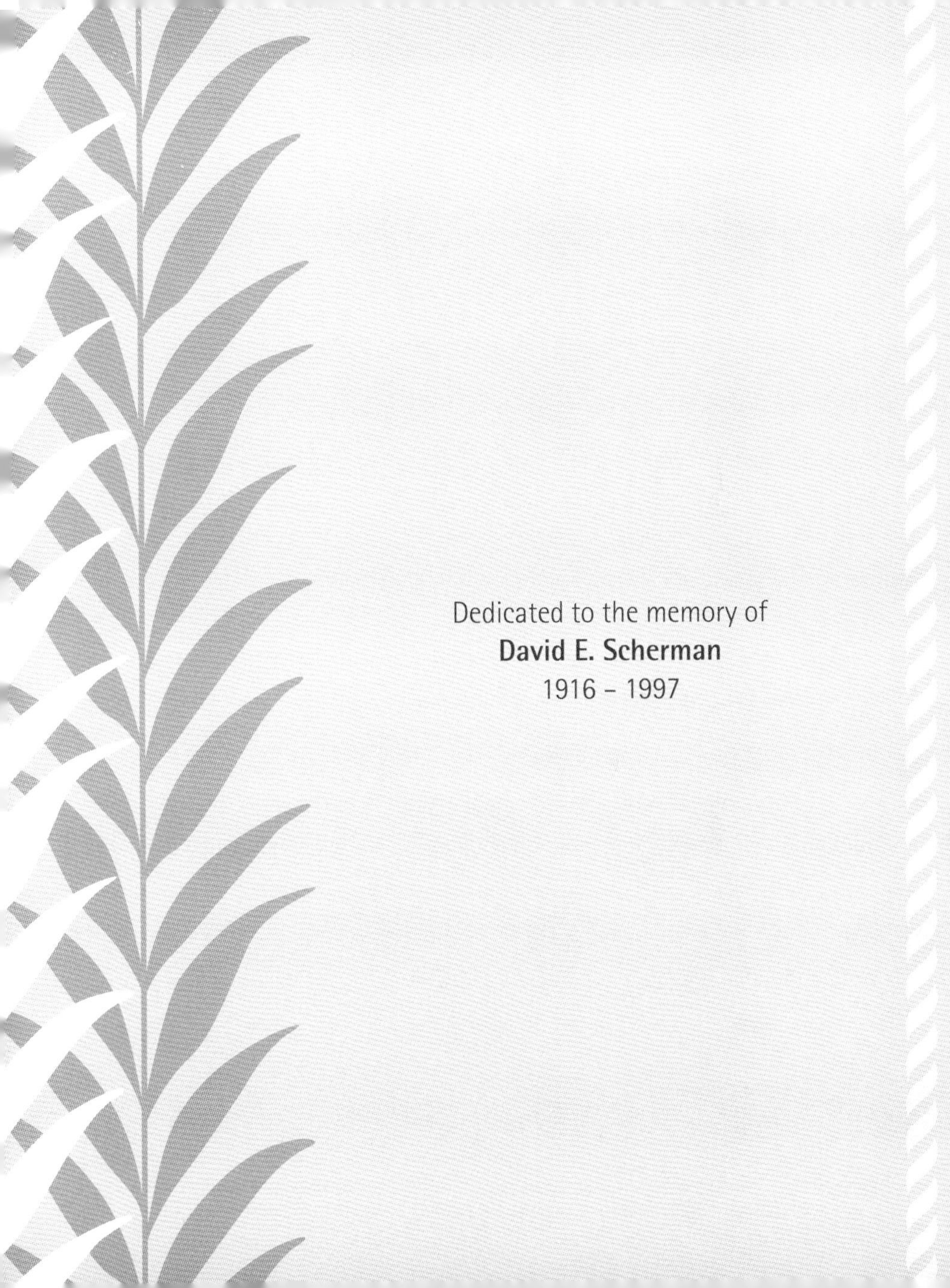

Dedicated to the memory of
David E. Scherman
1916 – 1997

'Some of them are pictures I saw in my imagination just as I would a painting'

Lee Miller
New York, November 1932

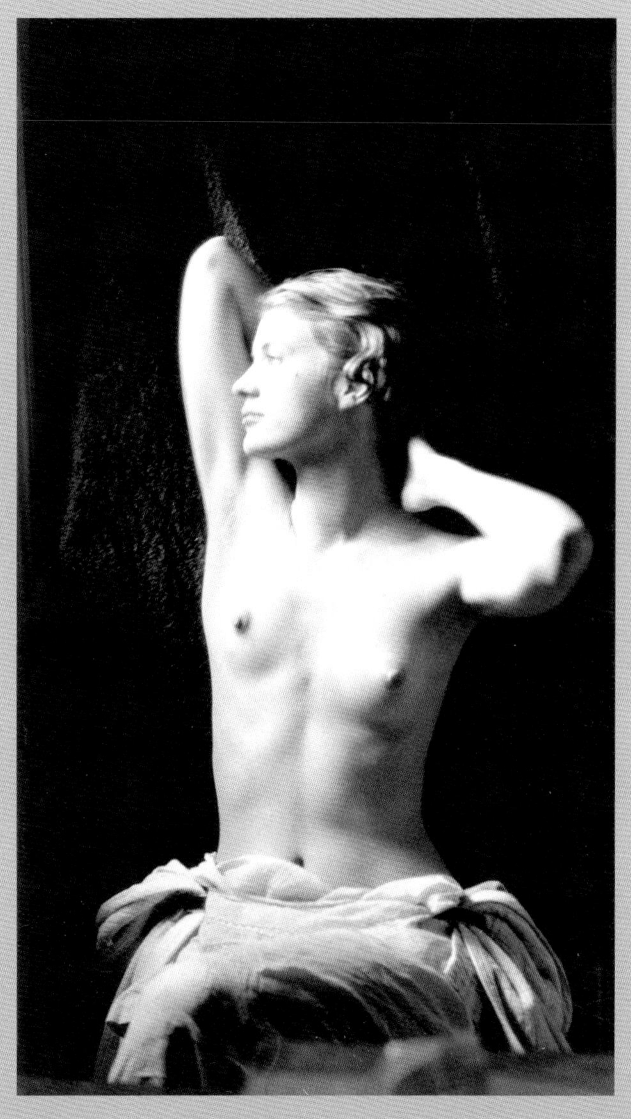

Lee Miller: Self-portrait, Paris, France c1930

lee miller®

SURREALIST LEE MILLER

By Antony Penrose,
Lee Miller's son.

Lee Miller Archives, Farleys House, East Sussex, England 2019

SURREALIST LEE MILLER

The first impression for people who met Lee Miller in the post war years was of a warm and friendly woman, intelligent, witty, but somewhat eccentric in her behaviour as was frequently evidenced by her wearing a toilet seat cover as a hat. Those who got to know her better found she had a darker side as following her war experiences depression and alcohol abuse had extracted a terrible toll, driving her to the brink of madness. She fought her way out of the main grip of these horrors, but they remained with her like shadowy tormentors to the end of her days, emerging as panic attacks or forms of egregious behaviour which alienated her from some of her closest friends and family.

Many people first encounter Lee Miller through the work of the American surrealist photographer Man Ray, to whom Lee apprenticed herself in Paris in 1929. It was his images from this collaboration that made some of the best known photographs in Man Ray's whole oeuvre. Her looks were fabulous, suiting the mode of the times perfectly, but the power of these images comes from more than his celebration of her beauty. They reflect the strength of Man Ray's relationship with Lee, a uniquely extreme and tempestuous love affair that endured nearly forty years, only ended by their deaths.

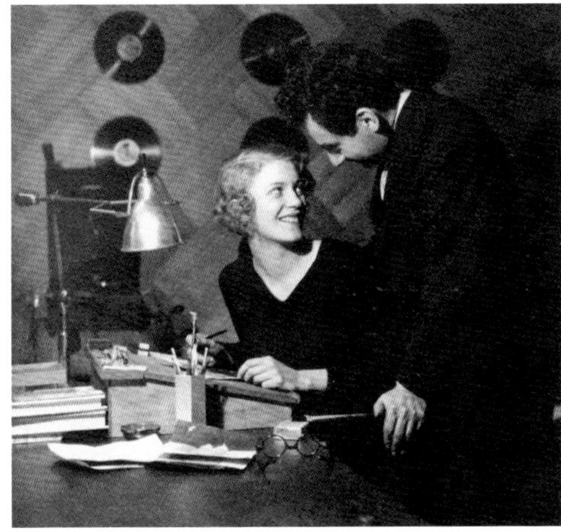

Theodore Miller: Lee Miller and Man Ray in her Studio, Rue Victor Considerent, Paris France 1931

On a page of his note book Man Ray's handwriting tumbles back and forth across the page in a wild swirling script – Elizabeth, Lee, Elizabeth – covering the mask like face of Lee drawn in pencil. On the back he wrote the legend:

Accounts never balance,
one never pays enough
etc. etc. love Man.

When I found this document among Lee's papers after her death, it had a photograph tucked into its folds. It is an image of Lee's eye, slightly larger than life-size. Man Ray's signature appears written with a sharp pencil in minute handwriting on the lower eye lid like a tattoo. It seems that in his bid to possess her he has left his mark on this most vulnerable and symbolic of places. On the reverse of the photograph he had written in red ink:

Postscript: Oct 11. 1932

With an eye always in reserve
Material indestructible
Forever being put away
Taken for a ride
Put on the spot
The racket must go on
I am always in reserve
MR[i]

The date was the day Lee Miller left Man Ray in Paris, boarded a liner and returned to New York. It was the end of a three year relationship that had trapped Man Ray in a frightful dilemma as a deeply committed Surrealist who espoused their beliefs. They claimed that along with all other bourgeois values, marriage was superfluous, families were redundant and free love – *l'amour fou* - was the only form of relationship that a true surrealist could aspire to. The double standard in this belief became apparent to Lee very quickly because whilst the men held they should be allowed to have as many lovers as they chose, they strongly disapproved of their women having the same freedom.

This hypocrisy did not impress Lee. She unknowingly had been a surrealist at home in America before the movement had a name. Right from the beginning she chose to live her life to her own standards, and that included treating her many lovers in what might be described as an aggressively masculine manner. It was she who unquestionably set the terms for her relationships, but she had to be discreet to avoid becoming socially ostracised. Her early childhood experiences taught her a lot about the need for discretion and secrecy.

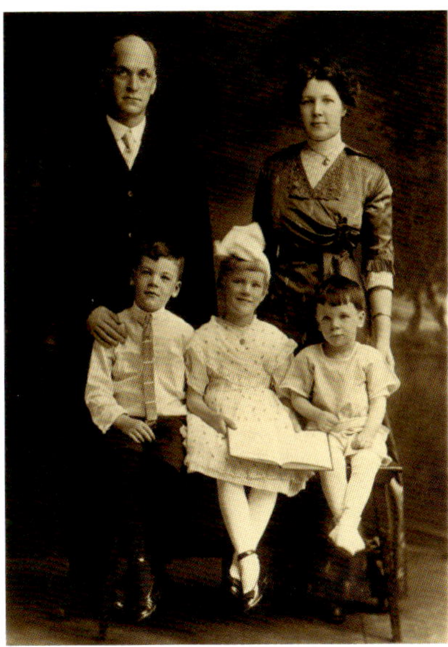

Unknown: Theodore, Florence, John, Lee and Erik Miller, Poughkeepsie, New York, USA 1912

Lee was born in 1907 in Poughkeepsie, in upstate New York. Her father was an engineer and her mother a nurse. There were two brothers, John, the older who became a pioneer aviator and the younger, Erik who became chief photographer for the Lockheed aircraft corporation. The Millers were a comfortably off middle-class family, but they had some unusual qualities. Theodore, Lee's father, adored her above all other members of his family, but saw no reason why she should not be an honorary boy, encouraging her to play rough and adventurous games with her brothers from an early age. Unwittingly he taught her to manage danger, a vital survival skill for her later as a combat photojournalist. He also cultivated her passion for chemistry and she learned the rudiments of photography in his own amateur dark room.

This seemingly idyllic family was shattered when at the age of seven, Lee was raped and infected with venereal disease. In 1914 the treatment was very primitive and painful. The task of administering it fell on Lee's mother, and the boys used to be sent out two blocks away so they would not hear their sister's screams.

Seeking to find some relief from the trauma of the rape, Lee's parents took her to a psychiatrist who advised her to look upon sex as simply a trivial amusement, and to reserve herself for love, as love was what really mattered. Love was to be held sacred above all else.

It seems Lee drew some comfort from this notion, but her life was brutally shattered once again when she fell in love for the first time with a local boy named Brad who everyone liked. They went out together on a lake in a canoe. He fell in the water and died instantly. It seems he had a weak heart.

Lee was utterly devastated, and similar tragedies followed. Among them was a young aviator named Argyle who was killed after he dropped red roses onto the sun deck of the liner taking Lee to France in 1929. It is probable that these tragedies caused her to form a huge injunction on herself against falling in love, lest it proved too dangerous for her loved one.

When Lee arrived in Paris on her first visit her immediate reaction was 'Baby – I'm HOME'. It was May 1925 and she was 18. The surrealist movement was emerging and the spirit of freedom it imbued must have reached her. She would have been drawn to their intention to break down social conventions, their new ways of seeing the world and of exploring the inner world of the subconscious through automatic writing and the language of dreams. This was underpinned by a desire for inclusivity and the passion for peace, freedom and justice.

Lee ditched her two aged chaperones and immersed herself in student Paris. We have no way of knowing if in that year she saw Man Ray's work in the surrealist exhibition at Galerie Pierre in Paris, hung with paintings by Jean Arp, Max Ernst, André Masson, Joan Miró and Pablo Picasso. It is likely she heard of him and maybe saw his exciting photography.

In Paris Lee found something she had craved during her formative years in America. She showed no inclination to return home, so her concerned father came over and dragged her back. There followed a period when she brought the stage lighting ideas she had learned in Paris at *L'Ecole Medgyes pour la Technique du Theatre* to Vassar College in Poughkeepsie but as soon as she could she escaped to Manhattan and enrolled in the Art Students League.

Her student life transitioned dramatically when one day she was saved from being knocked down by a truck by a man who snatched her to safety. He was Conde Nast, the owner of *Vogue* and *Vanity Fair*. He immediately recognised Lee had exactly the face and the figure he required and soon after she was on the front cover of *Vogue*, March 1927. She was not yet twenty years of age.

Edward Steichen, *Vogue's* chief photographer at that time, found Lee had the perfect looks for the period and his photographs made her famous as a model. Steichen adored Lee as a person and remained friends with her up to the end of his life. Ironically it was one of his photographs of her which ended her modelling career in America. It was used in an advertisement for Kotex sanitary towels, which when it ran nationwide throughout the United States in 1928 caused a scandal.

It was the first time a photograph of any woman had ever been used in an advertisement for feminine hygiene products and furthermore the advertising agency made up a product endorsement from Lee as a 'famous modiste'. This use of her image and her recommendation earned her total condemnation. Lee's modelling career came to a crash stop. No couture house wanted the Kotex girl modelling their fashions. Lee remained sanguine, stating she would rather make a picture than be one and used the event as an excuse to exile herself to Paris.

It was 1929 and Steichen gave her an introduction to Man Ray. She sought him out and became his lover, model and pupil. Her entry to surrealist circles was effortless but not without personal conflict. She soon informed Man Ray that if the surrealist ideal of *l'amour fou* was good enough for him, it was good enough for her too, and she was going to have as many lovers as she chose.

Jealousy consumed Man Ray and he became obsessively possessive of Lee. The short unattractive Jew from Brooklyn was stigmatised and subjected to the relentless corrosiveness of prejudice and countered this with a swagger. For him Lee held an importance beyond his love for her; she validated him. Of all the men in Paris it was he who claimed the attention of one of the most beautiful women of her time. Inevitably she could be regarded as his trophy and she rebelled. She was not going to be anyone's status symbol.

Despite the conflict of his possessiveness Man Ray was unfailingly generous with his encouragement of Lee in her photography. Her early works, many of them taken in the vicinity of his studio in Montparnasse, show that Lee developed a strong style right from the start. Here we can see what can be regarded as the key surrealist element in her work – the *image trouvé* or found image. Much is said about the surrealist *objet trouvé* beloved in particular of Man Ray. He had a talent for taking everyday objects and altering or simply presenting them in a manner which changes our perception of them.

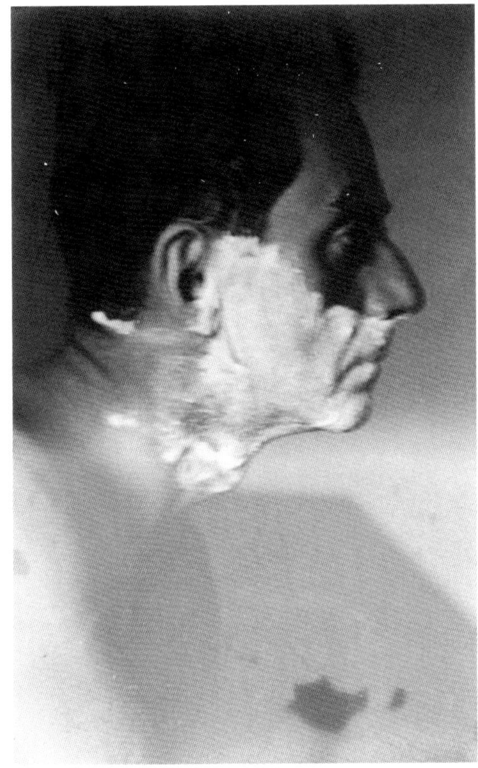

Man Ray shaving,
Paris, France 1929

Lee used her camera like a cookie cutter to snip pieces out of life, which in isolation assume a life of their own. Mysterious images appear, sometimes threatening, often abstract. There is no direct theme which links the images. They are moments stolen from time and place. They are *Images Trouvées*, Found Images and the counterpart to the much loved surrealist trope of the Found Object, something that already exists and demonstrates the finding of the marvellous in the everyday. We see these images reassembled in an order which Lee has no control over but that is entirely appropriate as randomness, chance and the excitement of finding unexpected marvels were the cornerstone of surrealist art.

Today it is particularly Lee's strongly surrealist images that endure with a fresh directness. They are there for you, the viewer, to attach your own meaning. Your interpretation might be that you find nothing at all or maybe you discover a rich metaphor, a visual pun or a fragment of a half remembered dream. In surrealism, there are no wrong answers for your interpretation. In this part of her work it was not Lee's intention to inform – her gift as a surrealist was to provoke and inspire us to find our own meanings in her work.

Another surrealist fascination was finding the marvellous in the ordinary and using it as metaphor. A wonderful example of this is to be found in her photograph of a mother and child in the waiting area of a clinic (page 48). The white clad figures in the background are a mural. The woman is real, so are the pushchairs and her baby, but the baby, being dressed in white, merges with the painted figures, a dream merging with life. This blurring of the distinction between reality and illusion is an essential surrealist trope.

It is hard to trace external influences on Lee's work. Her fashion and portrait work undoubtedly benefitted from her close association with Edward Steichen and George Hoyningen-Heuné when she modelled for them at *Vogue's* New York and Paris studios. Among other contemporary photographers she may have been influenced by the elegant abstract still life work of Paul Strand in America. She would have seen Edward Weston's semi abstract nudes in the photography press. Perhaps she saw the newly published portfolio of steel work images titled *Metal* by the German pioneer photographer Germaine Krull.

There is one known instance of Lee's work influencing another photographer. It seems surrealist Claude Cahun was inspired by Lee to photograph a self-portrait of her head apparently under a glass dome.

The dome is of the sort to be found in late 19th Century drawing rooms containing beautiful stuffed birds or other rare and fragile treasures displayed to enhance the owner's status. Beginning with a sketch, Lee set out her photograph. In her drawing the woman is a model with an elaborate floral decoration on her hat. For the photograph Lee discarded the hat and used her American friend Tanja Ramm, a woman of great beauty, who modelled for Mainbocher. The pose immediately gives us a captive woman, crushed and hermetically imprisoned behind the glass; her head displayed like a hunter's trophy. This metaphor must have resonated deeply with Lee who found herself besieged by men wanting to capture and display her. It is ironic that Man Ray, whose intense possessiveness infuriated Lee, shared the session with Lee. He photographed Tanja with her head imprisoned under the dome, blindfolded, to further emphasise her enforced helpless submission. He later published this photograph in *Le Surrealism au Service de la Revolution*[ii] titled *Hommage â D.A.F. de Sade*[iii].

Twenty years later Man Ray repeated the same image in his painting titled *Aline et Valcour 1950*[iv]. The recurrent theme of the captivity and oppression of women in Man Ray's work forms a paradox to the importance that he and the surrealists placed on the freedom of the individual. It may be that in Lee's work the frequent occurrence of images showing a longing for freedom derives from her making counterpoint to the extreme possessiveness Man Ray and others.

Cahun frequented Montmartre where Lee and Man Ray worked. She knew Man Ray and probably met Lee herself. In Cahun's 1932 version of the photograph her head is under a similar dome. Her is gaze is coolly defiant as if to state that though she might be a prisoner, she will never be a possession.

Lee herself would have been reluctant to admit being influenced by anyone – she despised copying and believed strongly in the importance of originality although in retrospect it becomes evident she and others occasionally appropriated ideas or techniques. It seemed this was acceptable if it was a radical adaptation rather than a copy.

In return for Man Ray's tuition Lee modelled for some of his most important works in such a way that we can detect the crossover from the necessary passivity of a model to the contribution of an artistic collaborator. Lee always wanted an active part in whatever was going on. Never passive, her insatiable curiosity demanded her total immersion in the work. When we look at her work with Man Ray we can almost hear a dialogue going on – the exchange of suggestions, ideas being developed, accidental discoveries made and opportunities grasped, until the end result was far greater than the sum of their two individual contributions. It was a mutual exchange of inspiration.

Inspiration can take many forms. It is safe to say Lee was the inspirer if not the inventor of the technique Man Ray named 'solarisation' (page 60). She later wrote[v] that she was working in Man Ray's dark room developing some glass plate negatives of a nude against a black background. A rat ran over her foot and she let out a scream and turned on the white light. Man Ray, seeing the plates in the developer exposed to the light, quickly grabbed them and dumped them in the fixer in an attempt to save them. To his astonishment he found the second accidental exposure had created the effect of reversing the deep black tones to become a light grey leaving a striking dark boundary around the light areas which gives the photograph its strange three-dimensional appearance, like a low relief. The result can give negative and positive in the same image, a truly surrealist effect. Man Ray was delighted, and they worked until they found a way to replicate the effect at will. He named the technique 'solarisation'. It is evident in both Lee and Man Ray's work, particularly in portraiture, and is the hallmark of their artistic collaboration.

Although Man Ray and Lee Miller fought many passionate battles over personal fidelity, they rarely quarrelled over the attribution of their photographs. Man Ray often used to pass photographic assignments to Lee to give himself more time to concentrate on his painting and Lee stated that her photographs were frequently published attributed to Man Ray. From Lee's own writing[vi] we know that although all of the images in the *L'Electricité*[vii] folio are credited to Man Ray some are by Lee but alas we do not know for certain which ones they are.

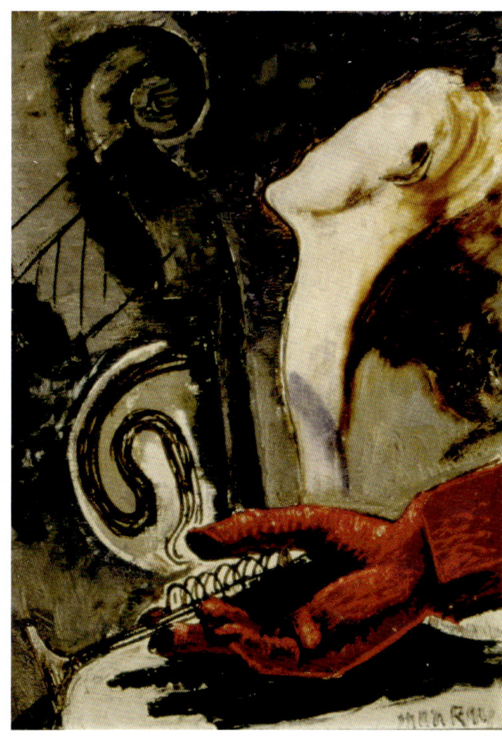

Man Ray: Le Logis de l'Artiste, 1931

Lee remained notably unruffled by the wrong attribution of her work, saying "we were so close it was as though we were the same person".[viii] There was however one momentous occasion when they did quarrel over attribution in a big way, and poetically the cause was a photograph of Lee's neck. May Ray was disappointed with his photograph and discarded the negative. Lee fished it out of the rubbish bin and worked on the print until she achieved the result she wanted. She took it to Man Ray who admired it greatly. And then the fight started. Whose work was it? Was it Lee's because she had made the print from a discarded negative, or Man

Ray's because he shot the picture in the first place? Lee stormed out of the studio. A few days later she returned while Man Ray was out and found the photograph pinned to the wall. The taut skin of the tender throat had been slashed by a razor and red ink cascaded down from the cut.

Sometime later Man Ray painted *Le Logis de l'Artiste*[ix]. In the background we see the stairs leading to the first floor of his studio. There is a hand, which appears in one of his photographs. It is a wooden hand, from an earlier work and it is holding a valve from a car engine. Man Ray liked including detached hands in his work. The pun on the French for hand – *'main'* – connected with 'Man', his name. Then there is the neck of a double base, another of Man Ray's recurring motifs, and unmistakably we see beside it the image in the photograph, the neck of Lee Miller, arched, her skin taut and vulnerable, with the gash across her jugular vein smeared with blue blood.

Many Ray's inclusion of this image of Lee as one of his possessions displayed in his studio like a trophy could be more revealing than he intended. Perhaps it signifies his desire to reduce her to an object over which he could have unchallenged possession and control to the point of fatal destruction.

Certainly the visual dismemberment of Lee's body is a significant and recurring aspect of his style. Some of his strongest artistic photographs are of parts of her body. Her lips, neck and eyes recur in isolation, and her torso appears tenderly dappled by the shadow of the net curtains that heighten the sensuality of her curves by providing us with a contour map of her body. But her head is sheared off, its absence depriving her of her individuality and reducing her to an object devoid of intelligence and unable talk back. She has become a beautiful, inanimate, erotic object.

The original photograph is part of a series where Lee was to have her head in images showing a rare sense of tenderness and lyricism. They are the work of a lover photographing his loved one eloquently communicating the love Man Ray felt for Lee. However the best known version that bears his signature is the headless crop.

The object which has become Man Ray's leitmotif has another dismembered part of Lee's body as a key component – the eye pasted to the bob weight of the metronome titled *Object to be Destroyed*[x] 1923 – 1958.

The awful challenge of trying to gain possession of Lee nearly destroyed Man Ray. The end of the affair came when Lee left Paris hurriedly in October 1932 and returned to New York. On the night of her departure Man Ray stood in the pouring rain in the Cimetiere du Montparnasse, howling his grief under the window of Lee's former studio.

It took Man Ray many months to expiate his grief, and his ultimate release from his torment was his painting *L'Heure de L'Observatoire*[xi], a pair of sensuous lips like the closely entwined forms of two lovers floating in the sky. They are the lips of Lee Miller, enlarged from a photograph. They are slightly tilted to enable them to fly in the serene dawn sky over Montparnasse. It was the moment when he forgave Lee and set her free, finally assuaging his grief at losing her. They were later to find a different love for each other that endured until the end of their lives.

In Paris Lee had found many other admirers apart from Man Ray. Among them, Michel de Brunhoff editor of French *Vogue* and Hoyningen-Heuné, the chief photographer who became a friend for life. Jean Cocteau cast her as the star in his film *Le Sang D'un Poète*, and she became close to Paul Éluard and Max Ernst.

The New York Lee returned to was still in the grip of the 1930's depression. It was the most inauspicious moment to start her own studio, but Conde Nast had not forgotten her and she had two rich young men as backers. She also brought with her a stylish Parisian chic which made her advertising photographs highly distinctive and sought after. She photographed in colour using the Tri-Carbro-Color process for pack shots and to save money she modelled for her own fashion work. The portrait clients began to arrive. People from the fashion circles, daughters of the wealthy and actresses on Broadway who wanted arresting images for sending to Hollywood casting directors. Then in what can be regarded as an enviable scoop, she photographed the entire cast of the opera *Four Saints in Three Acts*.

In Paris, Lee had met Aziz Eloui Bey, a quiet Egyptian business man who fell in love with her. He followed her to New York eighteen months later. They were married on 19th July 1934, and went to live in Cairo. Aziz (page 70) was no artist, but he loved her with patience and tenderness. To begin with she relished the highly privileged and sheltered life of an expatriate married to a rich man. Then she began to feel she was trapped in a gilded cage and sought relief by making long-range excursions into the desert with her friends and her camera. There was no commercial pressure or demands from art directors so her photographs from this period are her most striking and surreal. Some carry a sense of irony, like the sensuous breast-like domes of the Monastery of Wadi Natrun with the celibate monks living within.

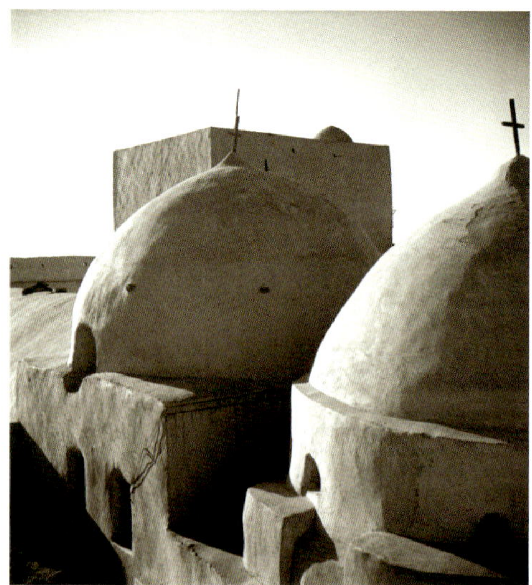

Deir El Soriani Monastery,
Wadi Natrun, Egypt 1936

Others speak more indirectly, like *Portrait of Space* (page 75), an enigmatic image that invokes Lee's perpetual quest for freedom which Magritte claims inspired his painting titled *Le Baiser*[xii], or the shadow of the great pyramid which stretches out over the land and the dwellings of the common people like the influence of the Pharaohs (page 81).

After three years not even the fascination of the desert could allay Lee's boredom, and Aziz indulged her with a trip to Paris. On the night of her arrival in June 1937 she met the man who regarded her as a surrealist woman incarnate and who described his first meeting with her as a *coup de foudre*[xiii]. He was quiet, shy and ineffably English and came from a strict Victorian background which had left him highly inhibited. He was Roland Penrose and Lee became his tutor in the study of personal liberation. Her photograph titled *Picnic* (page 78) shows what a repressed Englishman looks like when he is studying liberation seriously.

Taken in Mougins, on the Côte d'Azur, the others in the party are Nusch and Paul Éluard, Man Ray (in the white hat) and his new lover Ady Fidelin. They were staying at Hotel Vaste Horizon and among the other guests were Picasso and Dora Maar.

Picasso was so enamoured with Lee that he painted her portrait six times 'A L'Arlésienne' - dressed in the costume of a woman from Arles. Roland bought one and gave it to her as a present. He hung it in the sitting room at Farleys and as a child I endured merciless teasing from my friends who wanted to know why my mother had both eyes on the side of her face and demanded to know if she was really that ugly. As an adult I discovered Picasso had used a wealth of coded references that gave us a true portrait of Lee's personality as well as her appearance. He shows, the big gap toothed smile that Lee regarded as a blemish and usually concealed behind closed lips. Picasso had shown to the world like an emblem for her triumph over adversity.

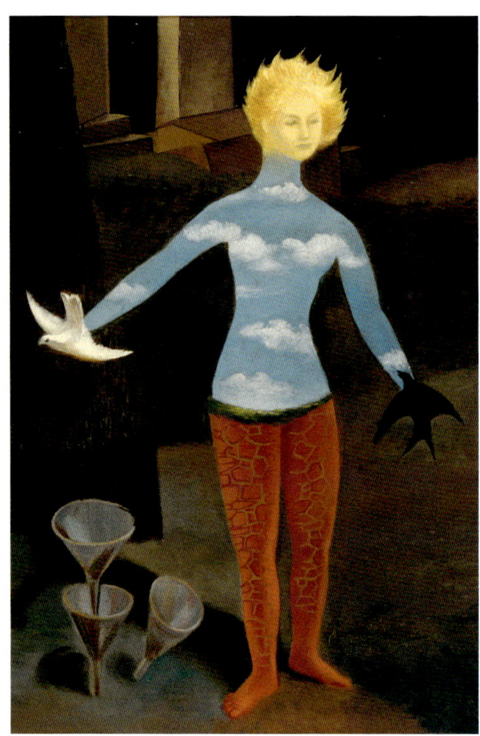

Roland Penrose:
Night and Day,
Oil on Canvas 1937

One of Roland's first portraits of Lee is a small canvas which he titled *Night and Day*[xiv]. Roland was highly intuitive and he once told me that he painted pictures because that way he could express things for which he had no words[xv]. Many of Roland's paintings contain a rich narrative of metaphors and my interpretation of *Night and Day* goes like this: Lee's legs are earth. As a person she was always grounded – strong and practical – earthy, you might say, although you should note that the earth is parched and cracked. Her body has become the sky. I think this is a reference to her dissociated personality[xvi], probably linked to the trauma of her childhood rape. It is as if she does not actually live in her body. So we have earth and air. Her face is like the sun, a metaphor for her searing bright intellect and radiated warmth. Earth, Air, Fire, but we see no Water. Water is often the allegory for emotion. Both Roland and Lee detested displays of what they called "sentimentality", so Roland has provided some funnels to catch any water which may appear and safely conduct it away to avoid embarrassment.

Lee left Aziz in 1939 and moved into Roland's house at 21 Downshire Hill, Hampstead, on the day the Second World War was declared. They married in 1947, a few months before I was born, and despite their marriage being fraught with extreme difficulties they stayed together until parted by Lee's death at Farleys House in 1977, thirty years later.

One of the most important people in Lee's life shared her with Roland for nearly four years during the war. He was David E. Scherman, a distinguished photojournalist for LIFE Magazine. After America's entry into the war in 1942 he was assigned to England to cover the war for LIFE's London bureau, following his brave and quick witted reportage of the sinking by a German raider of the ship *Zam Zam* which was taking him to North Africa.

Scherman (page 97) and Lee met as two Yanks in Britain, and soon with Roland's blessing Scherman had moved into 21 Downshire Hill and established a *ménage a trois*. Roland had recently been made a Captain in the British Army and was often absent from London performing his duties in the Eastern Command Camouflage School in Norwich. He recognised that Scherman was as dedicated to Lee as he and generously shared her, not wanting her to face the terrors of the Blitz alone.

Lee joined *Vogue* magazine as a freelance photographer, but bored to the point of stupefaction with taking pictures of frocks and handbags, she began photographing the damage done by the enemy bombs. Her surrealist eye clicked in automatically, and she produced one of her strongest folios of work. Surrealism has its roots in literature and poetry, and this influence emerges in the wit and irony of the titles Lee gave to her photographs. *Remington Silent* (page 91) was prized for being the quietest typewriter, but now in its destroyed state it is far from silent. In Lee's photograph it gives us thousands of words about the destruction of war. *Eggceptional Achievement* (page 89) is the title for two proud geese posing in front of what appears to be their giant egg but is a grounded barrage balloon. One of her best-known images for this series is *Revenge on Culture*, (page 90) the stone beauty who passively endures the brick crushing her breast and the iron bar jammed against her throat, perhaps a metaphor for the nightly torture of London during the blitz.

As the war continued and the US armed forces began arriving in vast numbers, everyone knew the invasion of France was imminent and Lee was terrified she would be left out of the story. The British Army would not allow women to be war correspondents so at Scherman's suggestion she applied for military accreditation with the US Army. Lee was soon equipped with a chic American uniform (page 96) and her own AGO pass card[xvii] which gave her privileged access to military areas.

Her first European assignment came six weeks after D-Day, and she flew into France to do a story on the US army casualty evacuation hospital at Bricqueville, inland from Omaha beach.

On her return to England she filed about 35 rolls of film, but more importantly, the woman who had never previously written filed a full length assignment of nearly ten thousand words of the kind of reporting that established her domination of *Vogue* features for the next year and a half. She had penetrated to the furthest reaches of her assignment, visiting casualty clearing stations close to the enemy lines, and her photographs show a strong sense of human compassion for the wounded and their carers. Lee was seldom interested in the Generals and the top brass of the rear echelons – she wanted to be where the action was and she felt at her most comfortable with the ordinary soldiers – she valued the integrity and tough directness of the people who were doing the dangerous, dirty work and she identified strongly with them. (pages 100 and 101)

A few weeks after filing the Normandy Nurses story, Lee was back in France, this time covering the Seige of St. Malo. The area was supposed to have been taken by the US Army but the German commander Col. Von Aulock and his forces still held the chain of fortresses that guarded the port. Lee defied the ban on women journalists entering combat zones and she stayed with the US 83rd division for the next four and a half days of intense fighting. In this moment she became a combat photojournalist. She witnessed an horrific infantry assault on the main citadel, the Fort de la Cité, which she reported like this;

The boy at the phone said "They hear airplanes". We waited, then we heard them swelling the air like I've heard them vibrating over England on some such mission. This time they were bringing their bombs to the crouching stone work 700 yards away. They were on time – bombs away – a sickly death rattle as they straightened themselves out and plunged into the citadel - deadly hit – for a moment I could see where and how – then it was swallowed up in smoke belching, mushrooming and columning – towering up, black and white (page 110).

Our house shuddered and stuff flew in at the window – more bombs crashing, thundering flashing – like Vesuvius the smoke rolling away in a sloping trail. A third lot! The town reeled in the blast – a large breach had been made – and we waited for the next attack.

I sheltered in a kraut dugout, squatting under the ramparts. My heel ground into a dead detached hand and I cursed the Germans for the sordid ugly destruction they had conjured up in this once beautiful town. I wondered where my friends that I had known here before the war were: how many had been forced into disloyalty and degradation – how many had been shot, starved or what. I picked up the hand and hurled it across the street and ran back the way I'd come bruising my feet and crashing in the unsteady piles of stone and slipping in blood. Christ it was awful.[xviii] (page 109)

It was indeed awful and served only as a small taste of the horrors to come. In the meantime there was a short respite as Lee arrived in Paris during the Liberation. She found her old friends like Paul and Nusch Éluard, Jean Cocteau (page 108) and Pablo Picasso (page 106), who whirled her off her feet, exclaiming, "This is marvellous, the first allied solider I should see is a woman, and she is you!"[xix]

Lee got a room in the Hotel Scribe, which was the Allied Press camp, and Scherman moved in next door. Together they followed the fighting across Europe, making such a formidable team that Marguerite Higgins of the *New York Herald Tribune* once complained bitterly to Scherman "How is it that every time I arrive to cover a story you and Lee Miller are just leaving?"[xx]

The list of their assignments reads like the battle orders of a famous regiment. Colmar, Neuf Brisach, Strasbourg, Luxembourg, Aachen, Cologne (page 115), Frankfurt (page 116), Nurnberg, Ludwigshaven (page 117), Leipzig and Munich. Through the winter of 1944-45 the allies fought towards Germany, repulsed the German counterattack at the Battle of the Bulge, and finally stormed into Germany.

Lee's surrealist eye was always present. Unexpectedly, among the reportage, the mud and bullets we find photographs where the unreality of the war assumes an almost lyrical beauty, sometimes with reference to other Surrealist artists such as De Chirico (page 113). On reflection, I realise that the only meaningful training for a war correspondent is to first be a surrealist - then nothing encountered is too unusual.

Lee and Scherman endured more than 30 days under fire and became battle hardened, but nothing could prepare them for the horrors of Dachau where they arrived on 30th April 1945, the morning after the camp had been liberated by Rainbow Company of the US 45th Division. Lee photographed, consumed with an icy rage as she thrust her lens into the battered faces of the captured German guards (page 118). Many of her friends were Jews, artists, or political dissidents who had undoubtedly ended their lives here or in similar places. The way in which she photographed the piles of corpses in close up (page 121) suggests she was searching their faces, for her missing friends.

She moved fearless around the camp, passing to the furthest extremity where a train was halted in a siding (page 124). It had left Buchenwald some 30 days earlier with 3102 prisoners on board. The G.I.'s found only one survivor who they rescued from an open truck. Doctor Jacques Hindermeyer, a French medical expert who was there as an eyewitness, told me Lee took the photographs he himself could not take because he was too overcome with revulsion when the G.I.'s opened the door of a rail car and rotting corpses flopped out.

One of the most important parts of Lee's legacy to us is this sequence of photographs. Here she is forcing us to confront the atrocity of man's inhumanity to man. Her sense of mission is at its peak. In these images she is crying out to us in a voice with passion undiminished by time, imploring us to: LOOK! LOOK AND

SEE WHAT HAS BEEN ALLOWED TO HAPPEN. DO NOT FORGET THIS, AND NEVER ALLOW IT TO HAPPEN AGAIN. Her imperative is incumbent on us all. Perhaps Lee was cognisant of the quotation from Edmund Burke (1729 – 1797): *For evil to triumph it is only necessary for good men to do nothing.*

That night Lee and Scherman found an exclusive billet in Munich. The city had run out of coal yet the banal apartment building of Prinzregentenplatz 16 still had hot water, so Lee took a bath (page 126). She was in Hitler's tub in Hitler's apartment. They set up the shot by carefully placing a kitsch sculpture by Rudolf Kaesbach[xxi] on the table, perhaps as a counter to Hitler's views of modern art as 'degenerate'. The vanity portrait of Hitler by Heinrich Hoffman had been the key Nazi poster throughout Germany and is placed as a snub on the edge of the tub. Lee's combat boots make the strongest statement. The dirt she is grinding into Hitler's clean bathmat is the filth gathered from Dachau that morning.

Lee and Scherman stayed a few days, looted some souvenirs, and then advanced to the front line at Berchtesgaden to witness the capture of Hitler's home and fortress at Obersalzburg. The retreating SS had set fire to the Berghof building and together Lee and Scherman witnessed what they later described as "the funeral pyre of the Third Reich" (page 127).

A few days later the war in Europe was over, and abruptly Lee and Scherman parted company. Scherman loved Lee passionately, he understood her perfectly, was the best friend she ever had; yet he could not live with her. He described being present during her creative process as like feeding his brain through a meat grinder. They toyed with the ideas for forming a journalistic team and travelling to other places but there was no real heart in the plan. Lee turned east to follow the G.I.'s to Austria and Hungary, Scherman turned west, back to Paris, London and New York.

Lee could not quit. She covered children dying in a Vienna hospital, watched helplessly by nuns because the gangsters had stolen all the medical supplies and she and the medical staff could do nothing but watch. She saw endless refugees, displaced people and freed prisoners of war trying to get back to their homes if they still had homes or even a country to get back to. She photographed the execution of Lazlo Bardossy, the Fascist ex-Prime Minister of Hungary (page 130). Not even witnessing the killing of Fascists alleviated the pain Lee was feeling. She began drifting and became ill.

Scherman sent Lee a telegram. It simply said GO HOME YOUR POSITION WITH ROLAND IS THREATENED. Lee went back to London, and the woman who had moved in with Roland discreetly moved out. Lee and Roland were reunited and Scherman remained one of their closest friends for the rest of their lives.

Vogue was grateful to Lee for giving them a voice in the war, but it became increasingly difficult to find peacetime assignments suitable for her. She could not force herself to settle down and take fashion pictures and celebrity portraits after all she had seen, although she did try.

Today we would call Lee's condition at this point Post Traumatic Stress Disorder, and much could be done to alleviate it. In 1945 the usual solution was called the "Stiff Upper Lip". Lee and millions like her were expected to "put up and shut up" and medicate the internal pain with alcohol. Lee entered into a downward spiral of alcohol abuse and depression.

It was cooking that saved her life, and probably mine too, as Lee suddenly developed her culinary talents. Surrealism hit the kitchen head on, and we had dishes like blue spaghetti, green chicken, gold meatloaf, beetroot ice cream and pink cauliflower breasts. Farleys House in the village of Chiddingly, East Sussex, which Lee and Roland bought in 1949, became a sort of perpetual arts congress with all the old friends visiting. Paul Éluard came alone. Nusch had died as a result of the privations they had suffered whilst on the run from the Gestapo who believed Paul's relentless insistence on freedom in his poetry gave them cause to murder them both. Max Ernst and Dorothea Tanning came. Henry Moore positioned his beautiful mystic sculpture Mother and Child 1936[xxii] on the lawn, and Picasso loved the farm so much he talked about buying one himself.

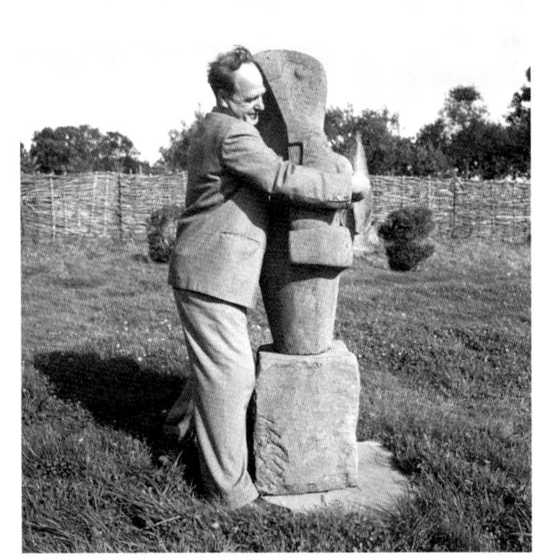

Henry Moore with his sculpture 'Mother and Child', Farleys Garden, Muddles Green, East Sussex, England 1953

My own experience of Lee was deeply conflicted. I grew up during the time when she was in great difficulties with depression and alcohol dependence, and became very remote from her. We fought like furies and if she alone had been responsible for my upbringing I would not have survived. Fortunately I was allowed to run wild on the farm and was brought up by our housekeeper, Patsy. She gave me the love and security I needed.

I did not know Lee during her lifetime – we were always embattled or she was someplace else, and I can say I really only discovered her through studying her work and piecing together her life, helped by David Scherman and many others. I have found her work has inspired me, and caused me to study things and meet people whom I would never have made contact with in the normal course of my life which for many years was as an English dairy farmer. My life is infinitely richer as a result of working with Lee's material which is ironic, because shortly before she died in 1977, I asked her if any of her work remained and if I could help her catalogue it. She absolutely refused, saying that nothing remained as everything had been destroyed and besides working with another person's material was likely to be detrimental to my own creativity. The latter may be something she learned whilst working with Man Ray, but I am glad I did not follow her advice.

Since Lee's death every year that passes sees her work more widely acclaimed. Exhibitions, books and films occur worldwide, and the story of her life continues to inspire people. In 2001 Richard Calvocoressi curated a major exhibition at The Scottish National Gallery of Modern Art titled *The Surrealist and The Photographer*. Roland was the surrealist, Lee the photographer. Mark Haworth-Booth's centenary exhibition *The Art of Lee Miller*[xxiii] presented Lee as the multi talented artist that she undoubtedly was, beginning its international tour at the Victoria and Albert Museum in London 2007. It was seen by more than 500,000 visitors and the show's last venue was at the Jeu de Paume in Paris, eighty years on from when Lee had arrived in that city to take Man Ray by storm. The success of her exhibition showed she had lost none of her impact.

Today she seems welcome wherever she appears and the aspect of her success I find the most gratifying is that her biggest audience sector for her exhibitions comprises of women, many being in the eighteen to twenty-five age bracket. It is deeply rewarding to find she is relevant to young people. She would have liked that. Another thing that would have pleased her is to see the way her close friends among the women surrealist artists are being recognised. Leonora Carrington, Nusch Éluard, Ady Fidelin, Eileen Agar, Dora Maar and Dorothea Tanning are celebrated with books, exhibitions and films. Lee would be especially pleased with Tanning's success as she remained resolute in her love and friendship during Lee's difficult post war years.

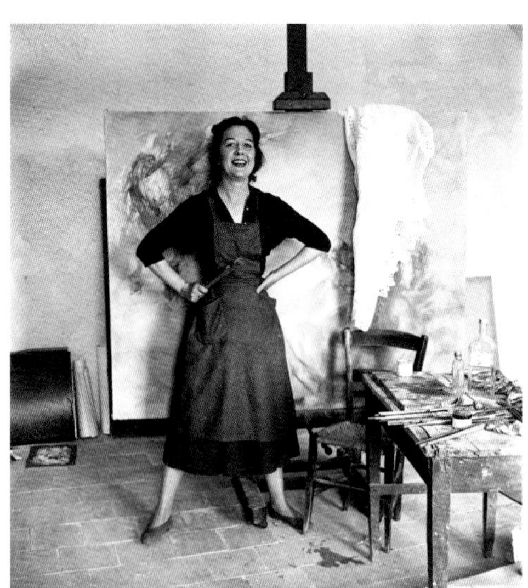

Dorothea Tanning,
Huismes, France 1955

FOOTNOTES

[i] Collection Lee Miller Archives, England.

[ii] *Hommage â D.A.F. de Sade* by Man Ray, published *Le Surrealism au Service de la Revolution* No 2 October 1930. Plate No 1.

[iii] The Marquis de Sade, much celebrated by the surrealists.

[iv] *Aline et Valcour* is also the title de Sade's novel of 1795.

[v] *I worked with Man Ray* by Lee Miller, *Lilliput* October Vol 9 No.4. P315.

[vi] *My Man Ray. An interview with Lee Miller Penrose* by Mario Amaya. *Art in America* May/June 1975.

[vii] *Electricité.* A folio of 10 rayographs by Man Ray and Lee Miller 1931. Commissioned by *La Compagnie Parisienne de distribution d'Electricité.*

[viii] Author's recollections of *conversations* with his mother c.1976.

[ix] *L'Logis de Artiste* by Man Ray Oil on canvas c.1931. Coll. The Penrose Collection.

[x] Following the destruction by reactionary students of *Object to be Destroyed c.1950* Man Ray subsequently made several further editions, re-titling the work *Indestructible Object.* An example dated 1954 is in The Penrose Collection.

[xi] *Les Amoureux or L'Heure de l'Observatoire,* Oil on canvas, 1934 by Man Ray. Private collection.

[xii] *Le Baiser* (The Kiss), Oil on canvas 1938 by René Magritte Collection: Musées Royaux des Beaux-Arts de Belgique, Brussels.

[xiii] *Coup de foudre.*(Fr.) Struck by lightning.

[xiv] *Night and Day,* oil on canvas 1946 by Roland Penrose. c/o The Penrose Collection.

[xv] Author's recollection of *conversation* with his father c.1980.

[xvi] Dissociation is a mental process of disconnecting from one's thoughts, feelings, memories or sense of identity. Most mental health professionals believe that the underlying cause of dissociative disorders is chronic trauma in childhood. Examples of trauma included repeated physical or sexual abuse, emotional abuse or neglect. Victoria State Department (Australia) Better Health Channel.

[xvii] The AGO pass was issued on 30th December 1942 by Adjutant General's Office and allowed Lee to enter non-combat military areas.

[xviii] The siege began on 3rd August and ended on17th. It appears from Lee's notes that she arrived on or just before the 13th. Her despatch was published as The Siege of St Malo in *Vogue* Magazine, October 1944, p41.

[xix] *Scrap Book* by Roland Penrose. Thames & Hudson 1981 p.136.

[xx] *The Lives of Lee Miller* by Antony Penrose. Thames & Hudson 1985 p.138.

[xxi] Rudolf Kaesbach 1873-1955.

[xxii] *Mother and Child* Henry Moore 1936. Hornton Stone. Leeds City Art Gallery.

[xxiii] *The Art of Lee Miller* curated by Mark Haworth-Booth. Exhibition tour schedule: Victoria and Albert Museum, London. 2007/2008. Philadelphia Museum of Art. 2008. San Francisco Museum of Modern Art. 2008 and Jeu de Paume, Paris. 2009.

SURREALIST
LEE MILLER

IMAGES

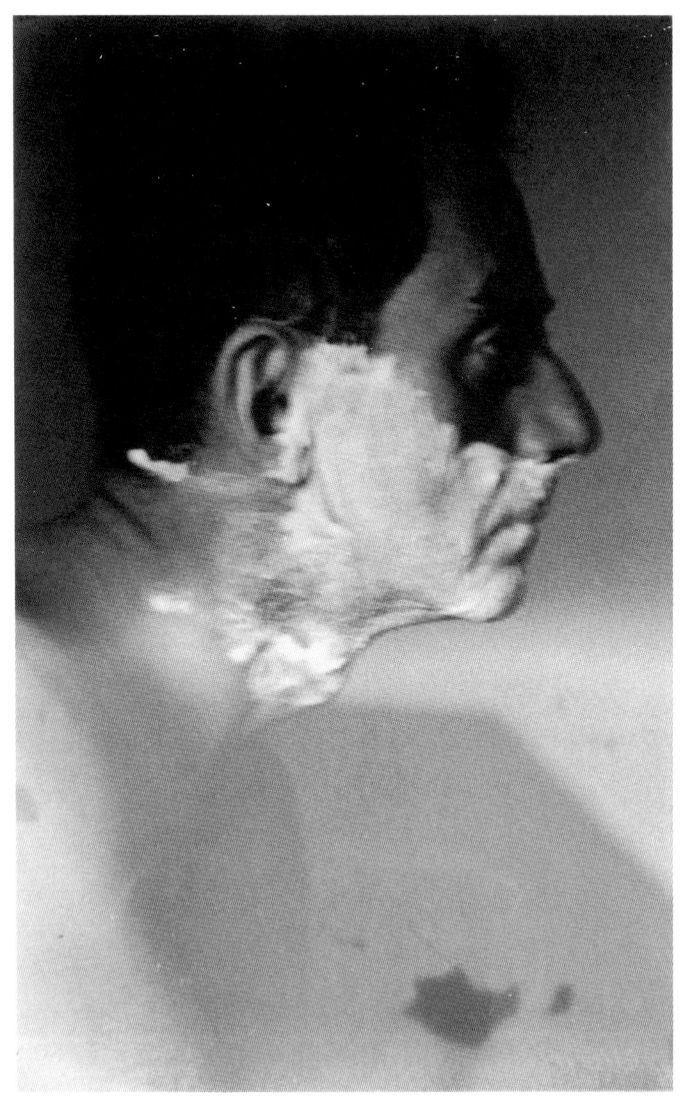

01 **Man Ray shaving**, Paris, France 1929

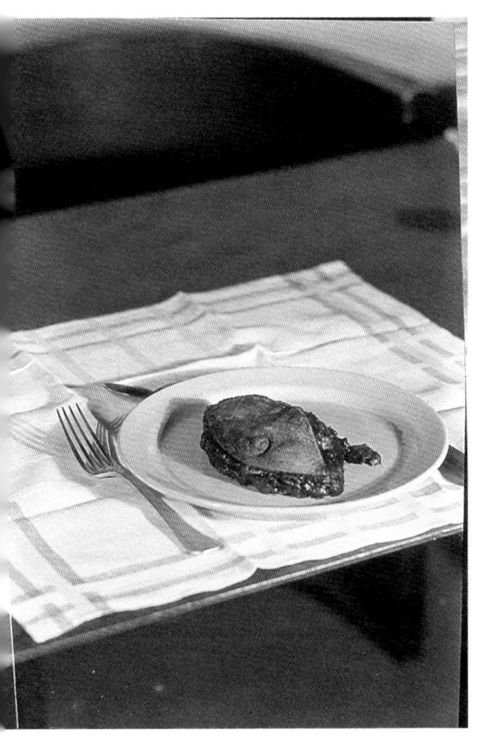

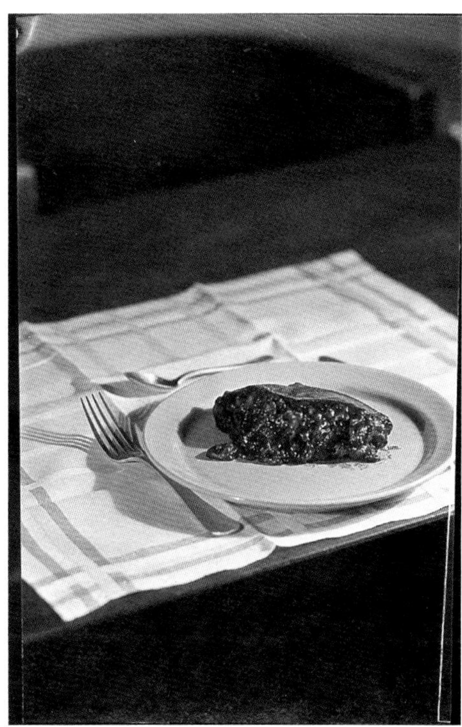

02 **Untitled [Severed breast from radical surgery in a place setting 1 & 2]**, Paris, France c1929

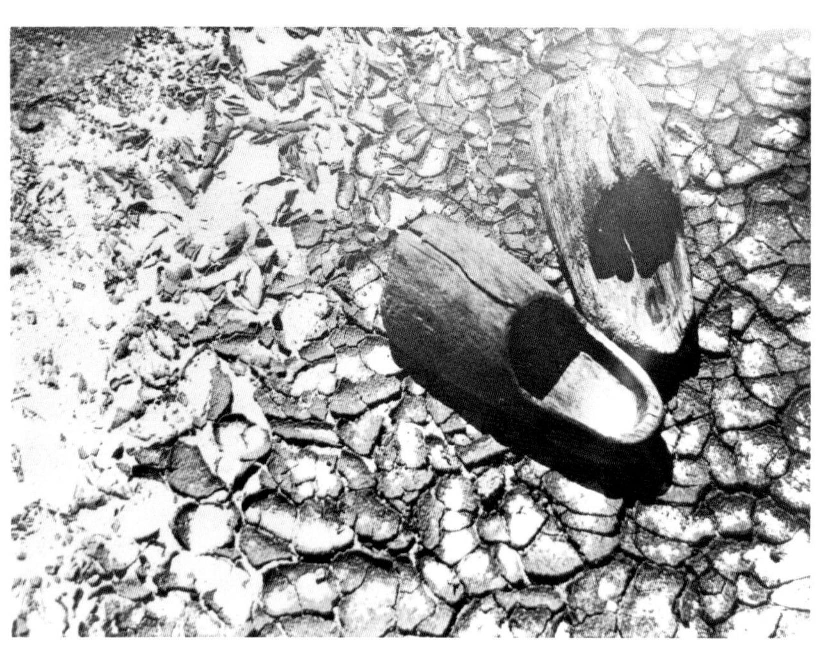

03 **Untitled [Sabots on parched earth]**, Paris, France c1930

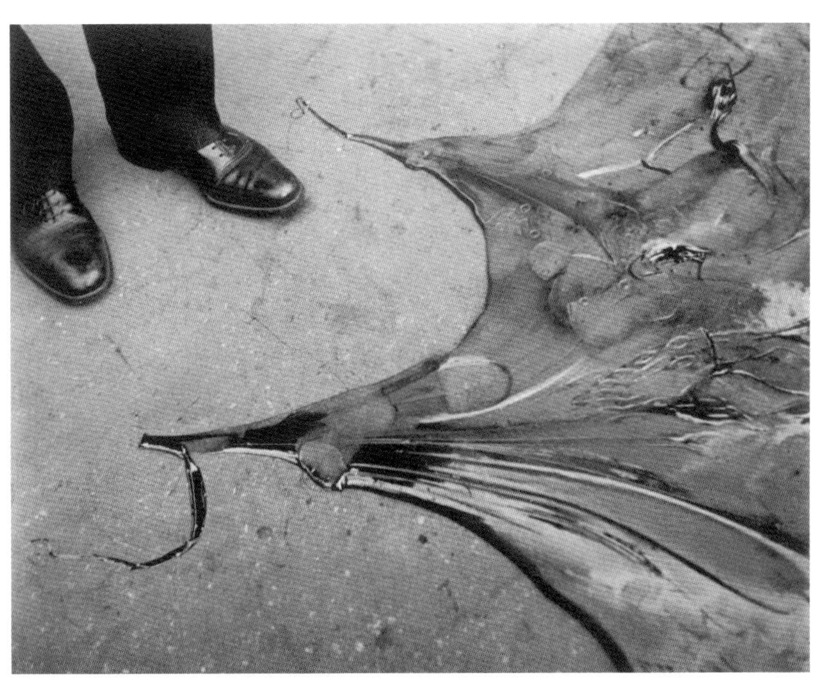

04 **Untitled [Man and tar]**, Paris, France c1930

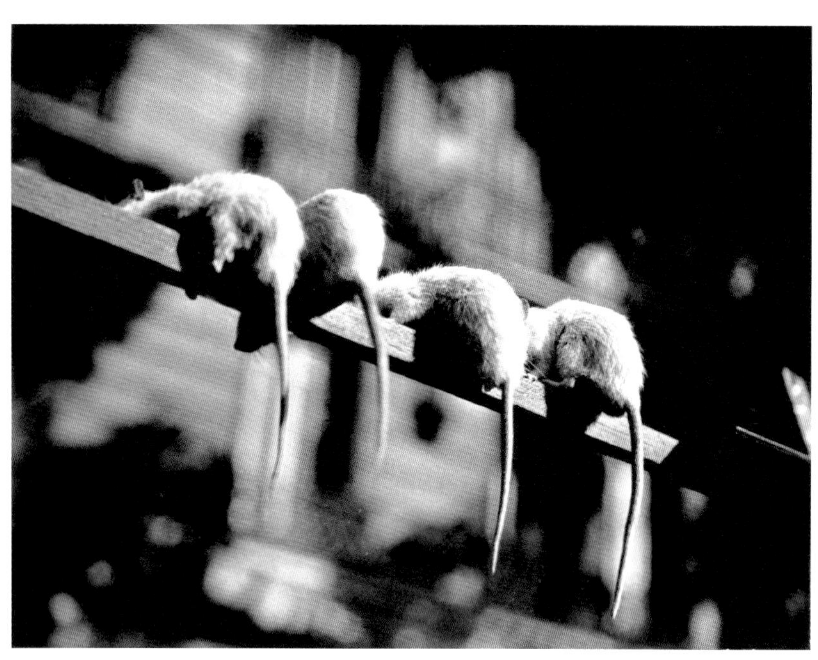

05 **Untitled [Rat tails]**, Paris, France c1930

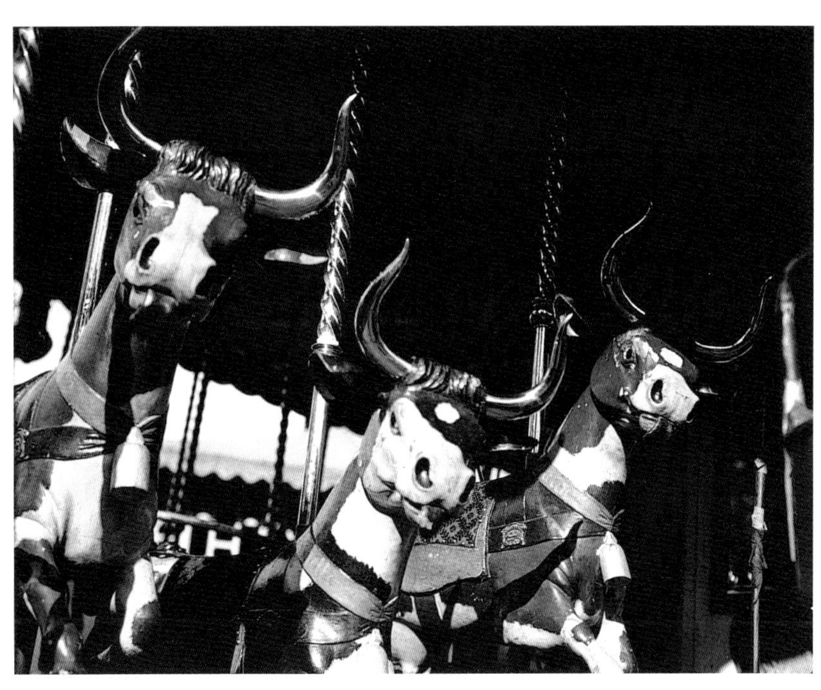

06 **Untitled [Carousel cows]**, Paris, France c1930

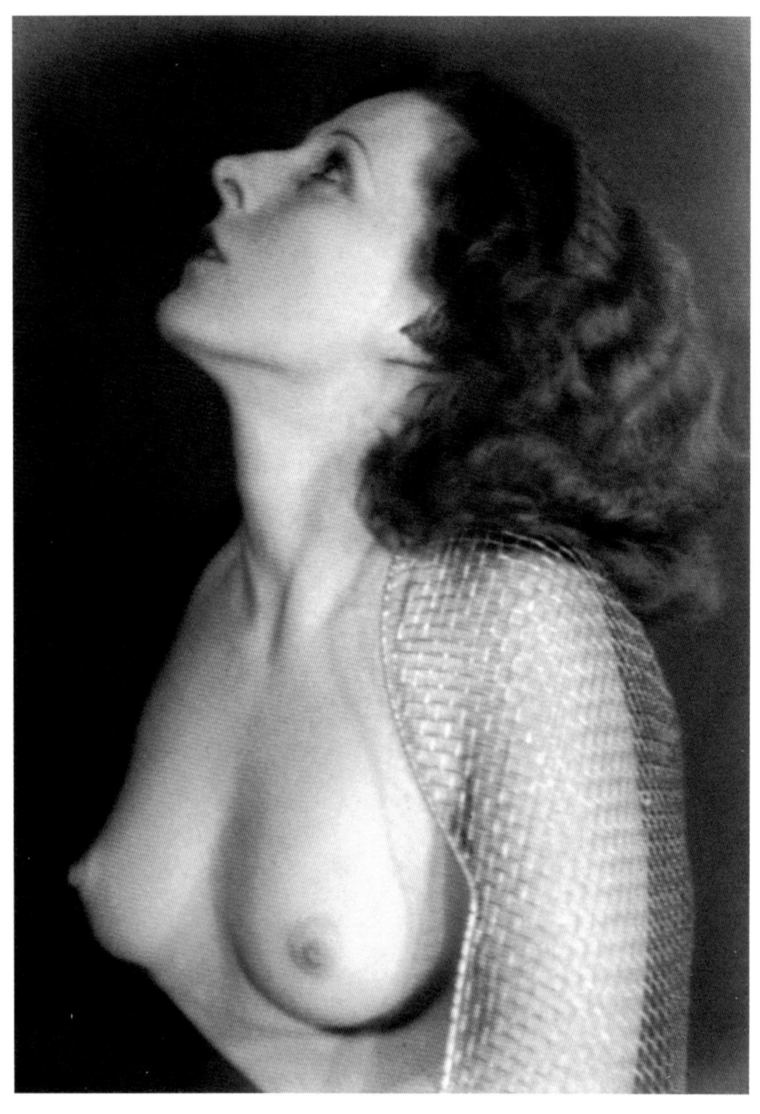

07 **Untitled [Nude wearing a sabre guard]**, Paris, France c1930

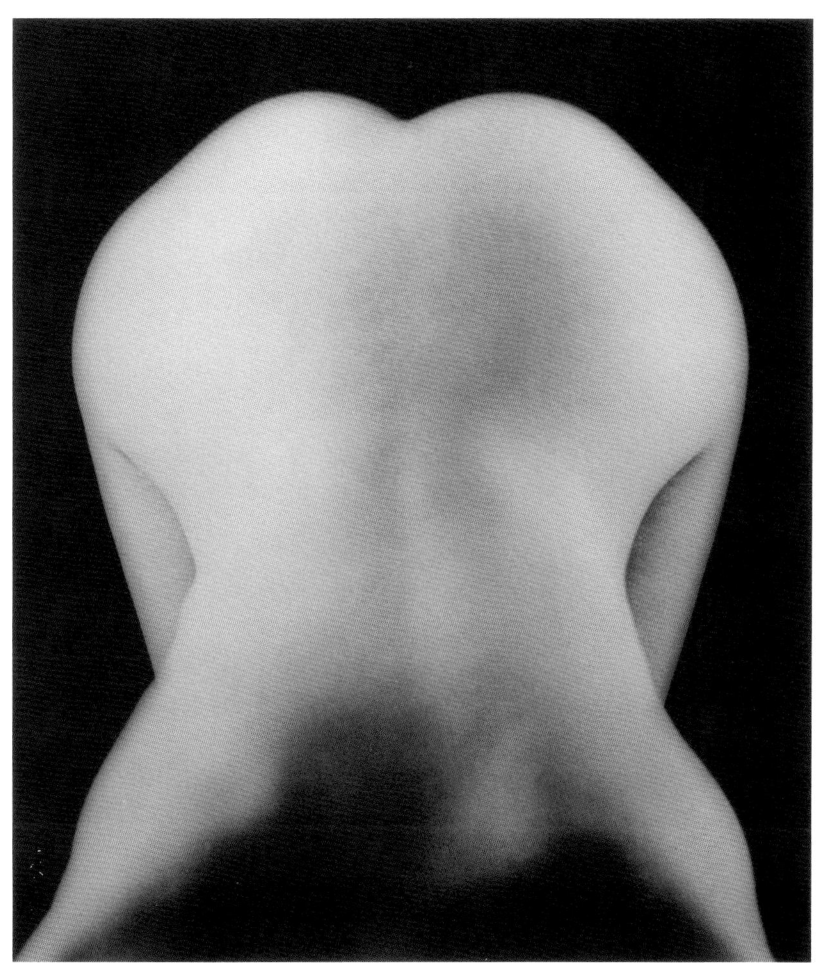

08 **Nude bent forward [thought to be Noma Rathner]**, Paris, France c1930

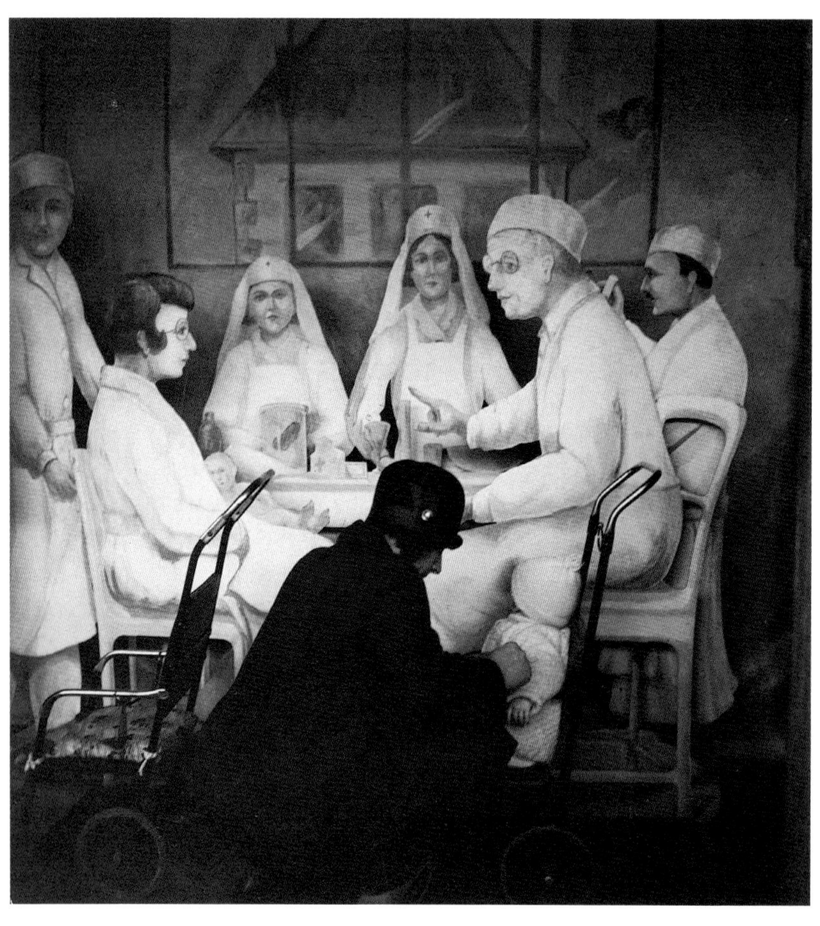

09 **Untitled [Woman and child in clinic]**, Paris, France c1930
10 **Tanja Ramm under a bell jar**, Paris, France 1930

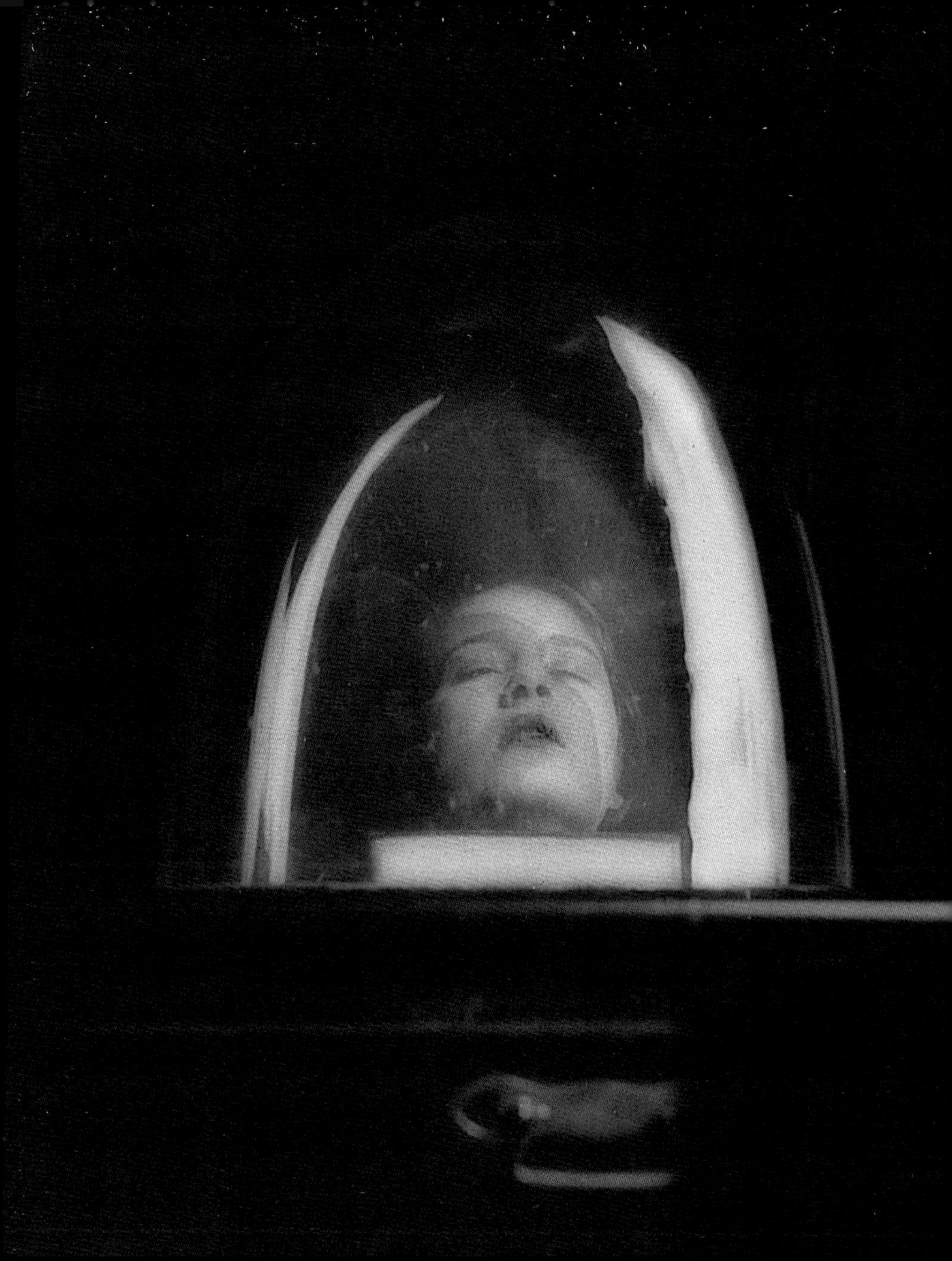

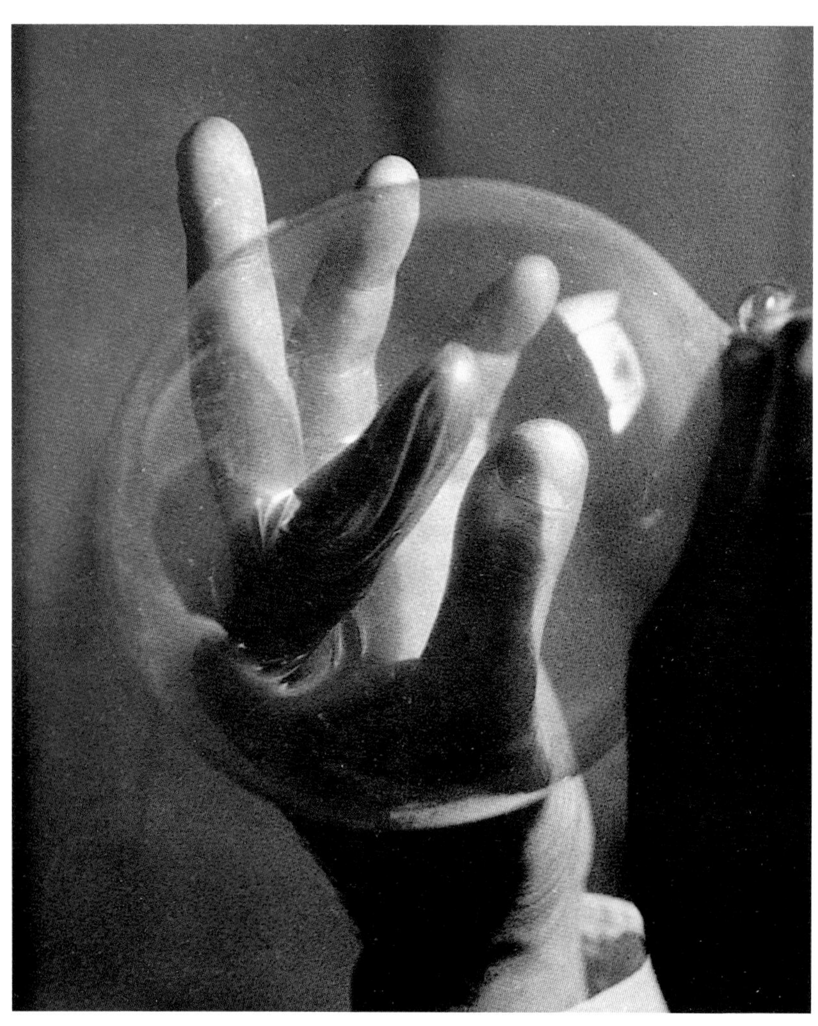

11 **Condom**, Paris, France c1930

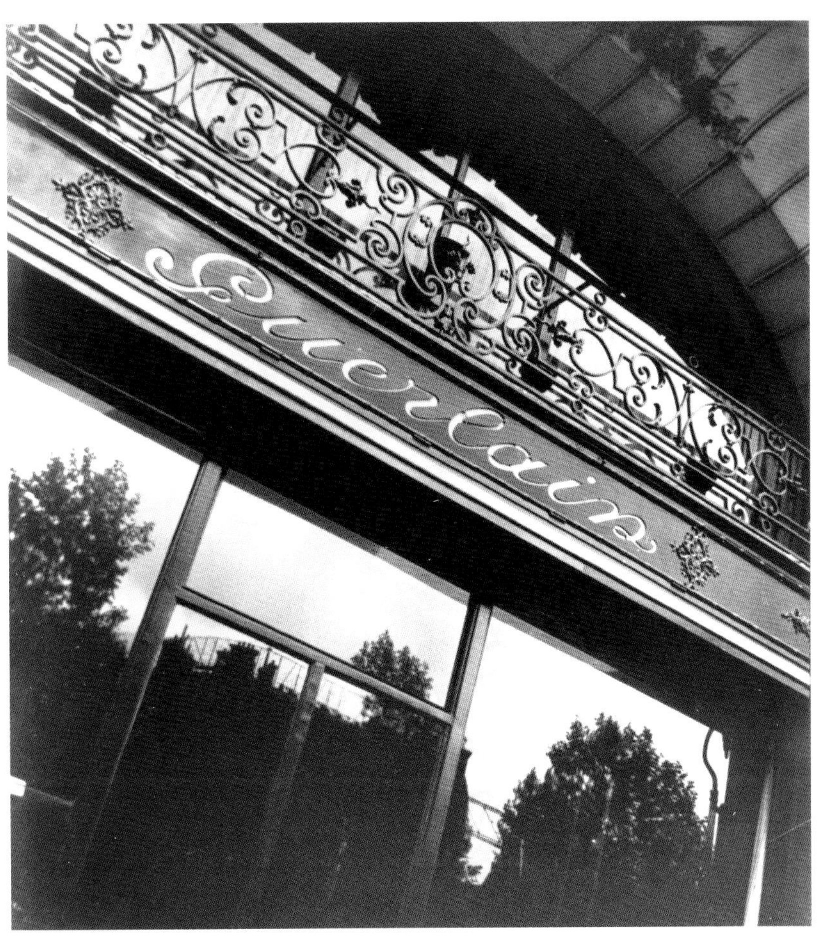

12 **Guerlain shopfront**, Paris, France c1930

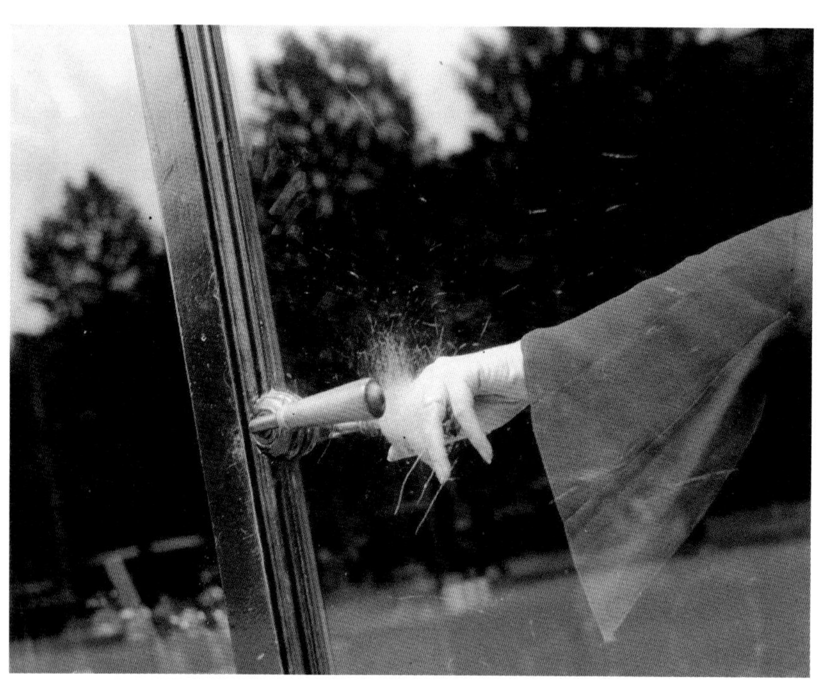

13 **Untitled [Exploding hand]**, Paris, France 1931

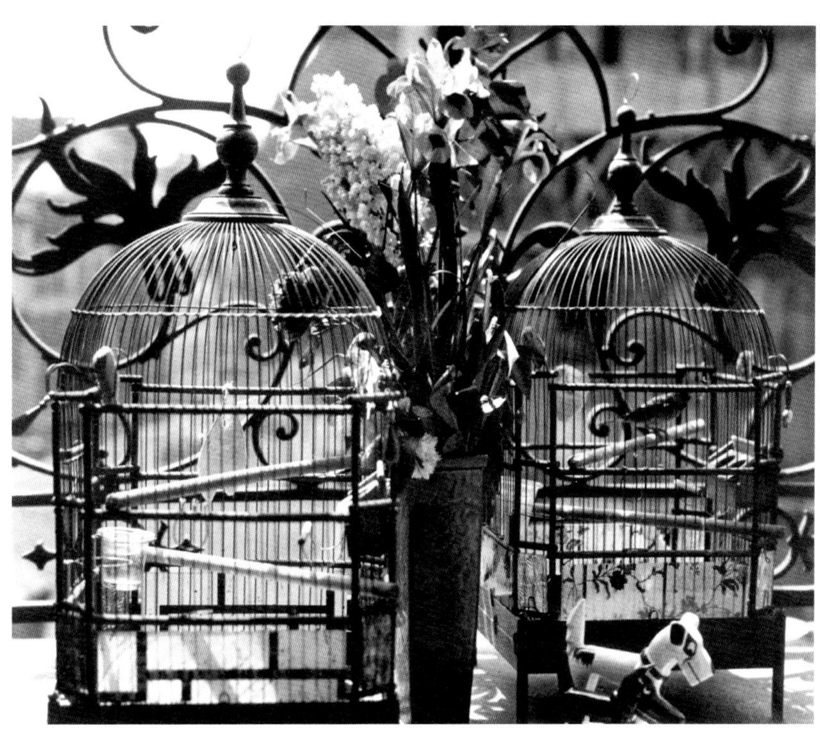

14 **Untitled [Caged Birds]**, Paris, France 1931

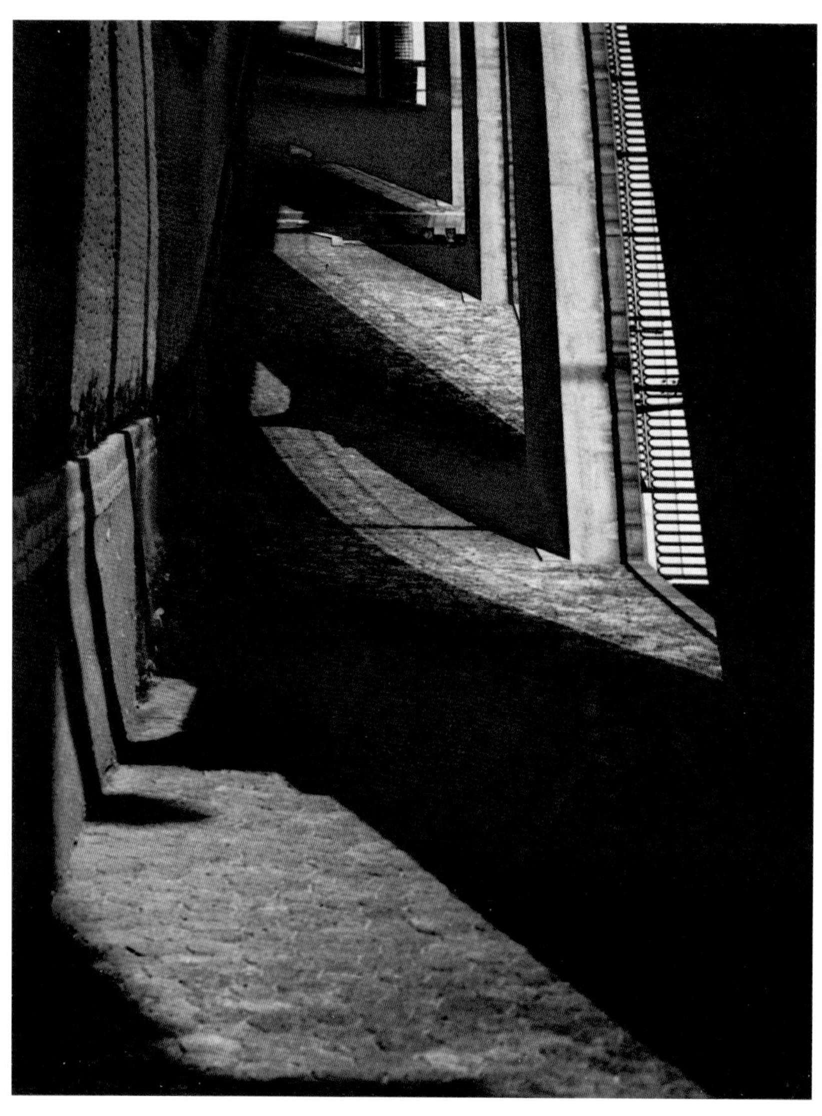

15 **Untitled [Impasse des deux anges]**, Paris, France c1931

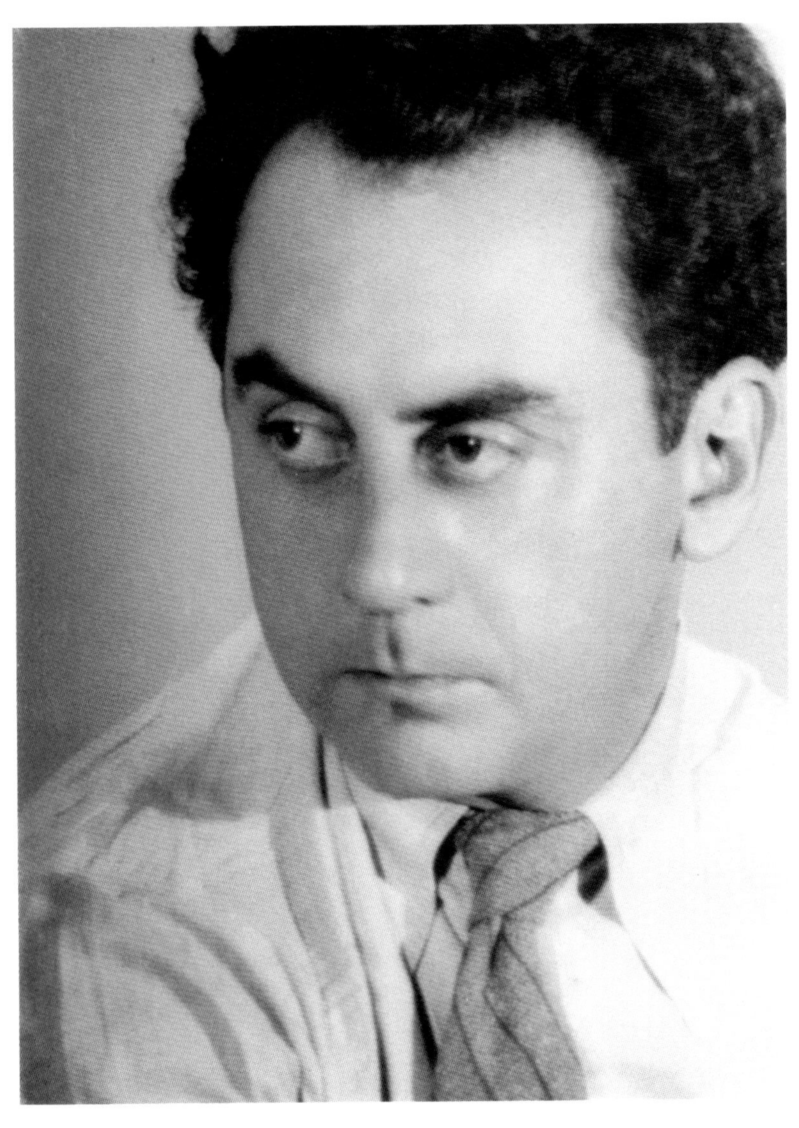

16 **Man Ray**, Paris, France 1931

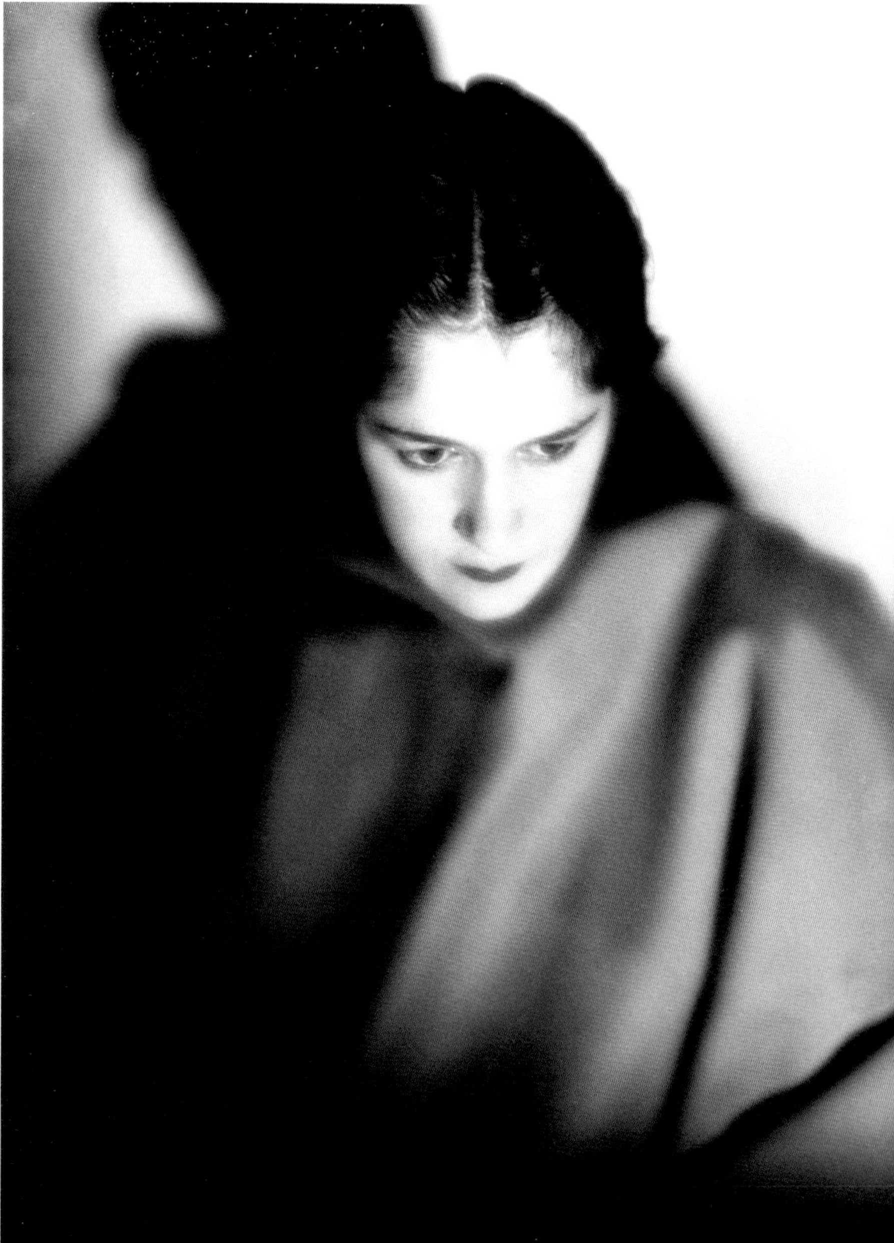

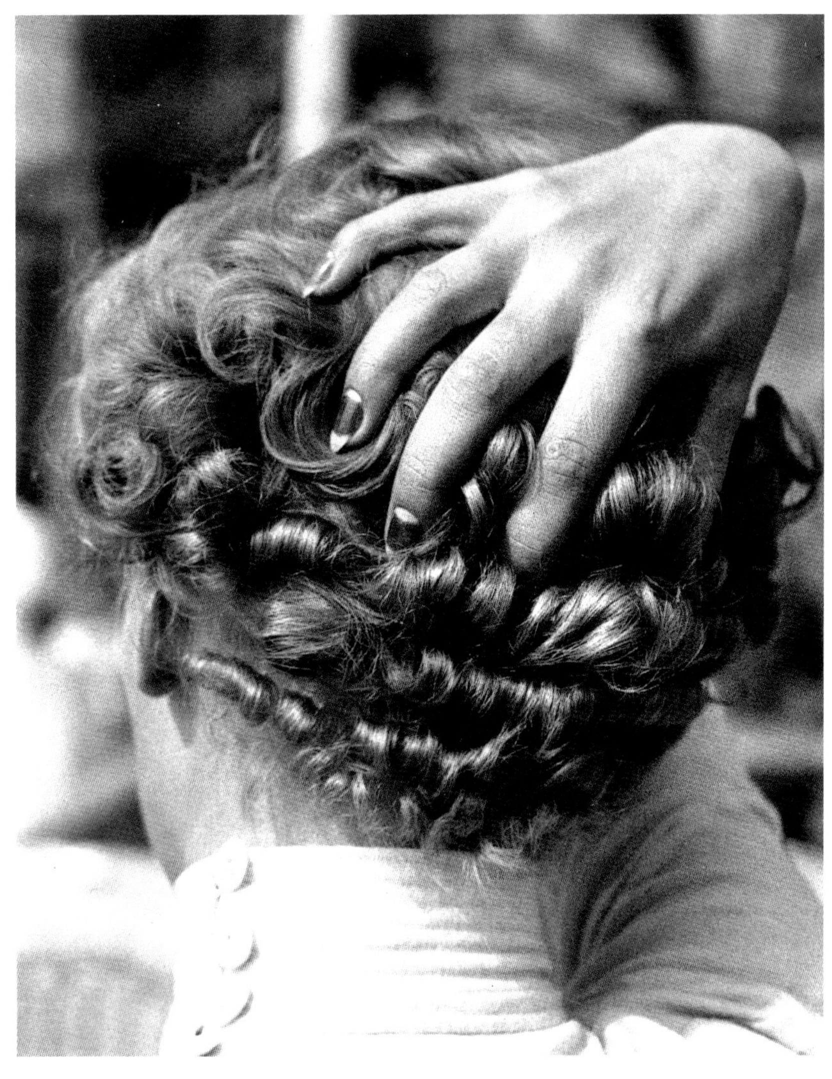

17 **Tanja Ramm**, Paris, France 1931

18 **Untitled [Woman with hand on head]**, Paris, France 1931

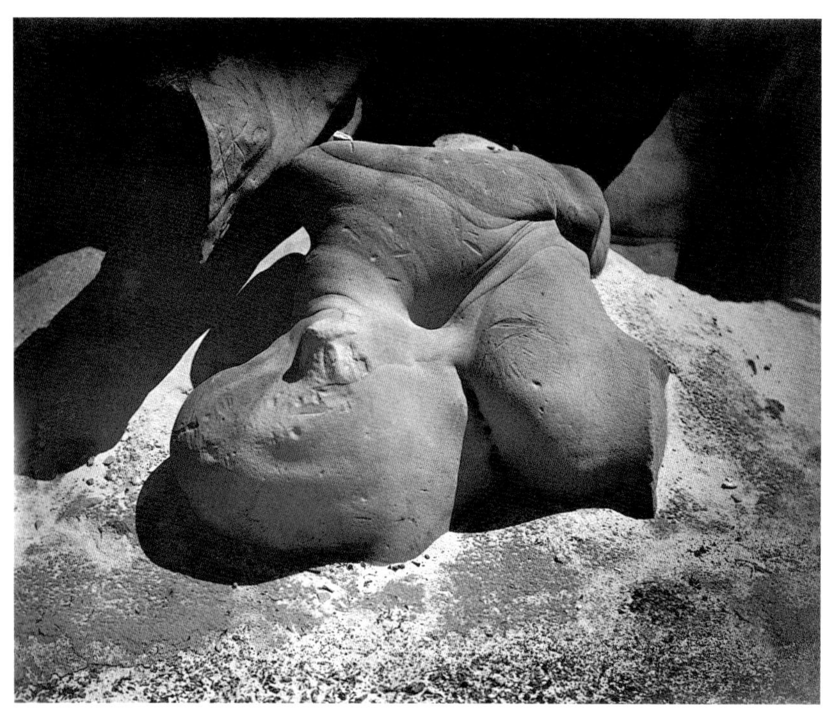

19 **Untitled [Stone]**, Paris, France 1931

20 **Untitled [Window]**, Paris, France c1932

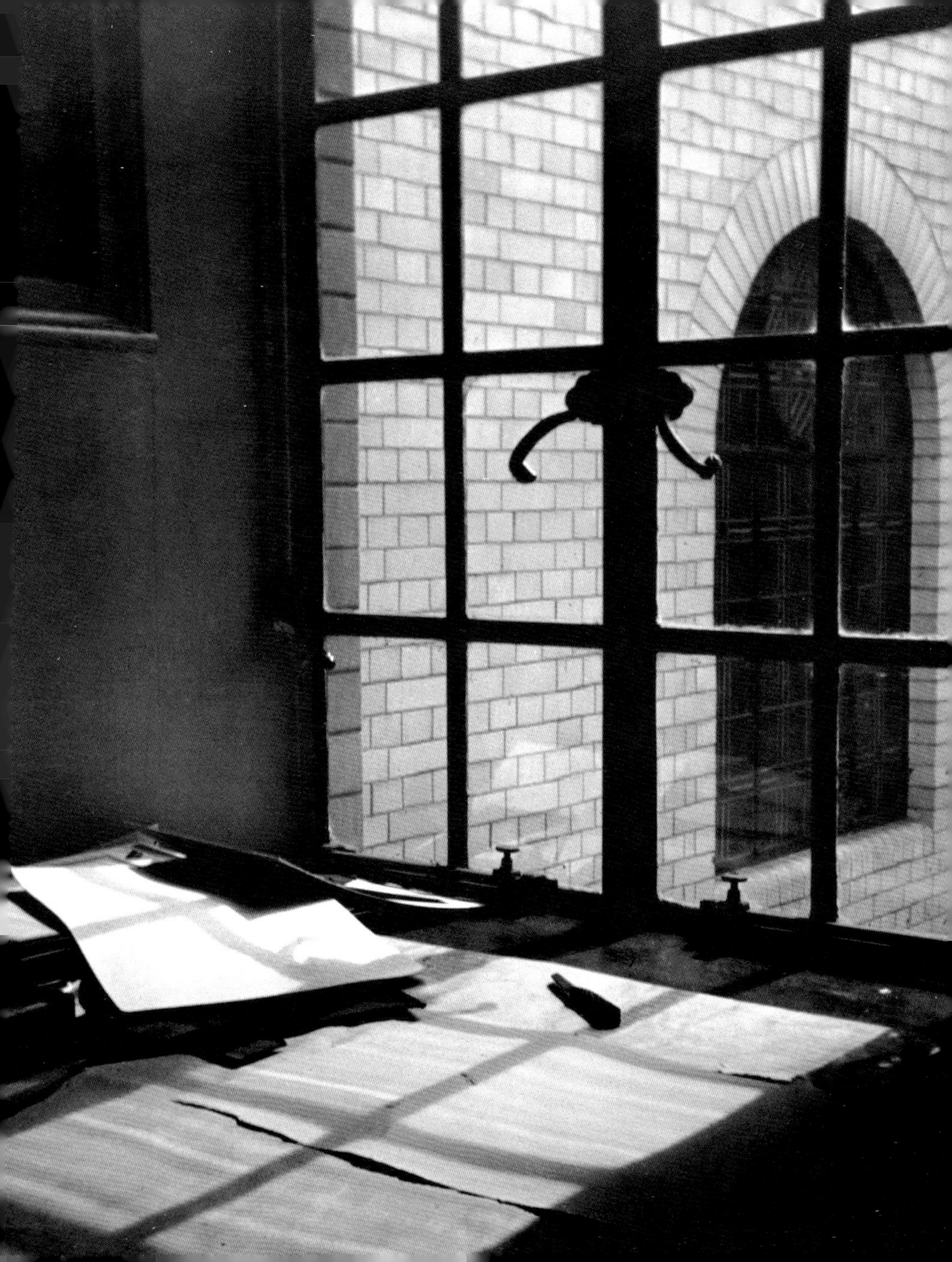

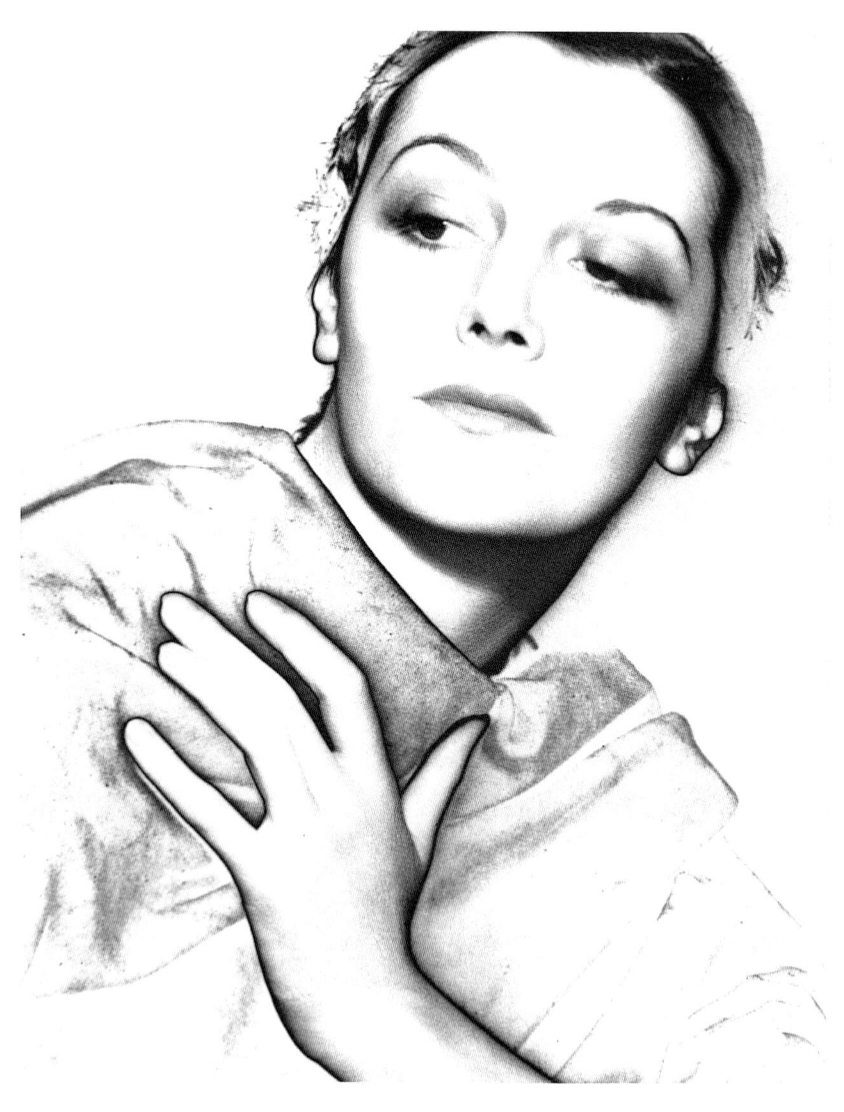

21 **Solarised Portrait [thought to be Meret Oppenheim]**, Paris, France 1932

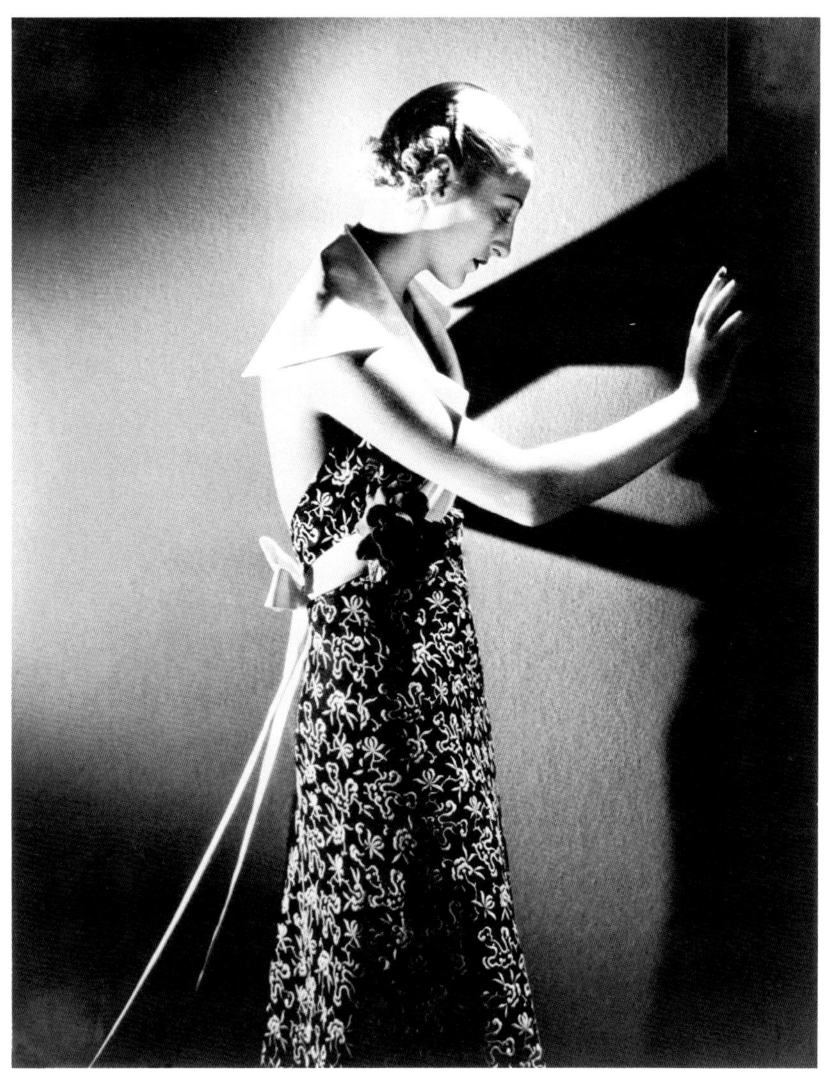

22 **Fashion study**, Paris, France 1932

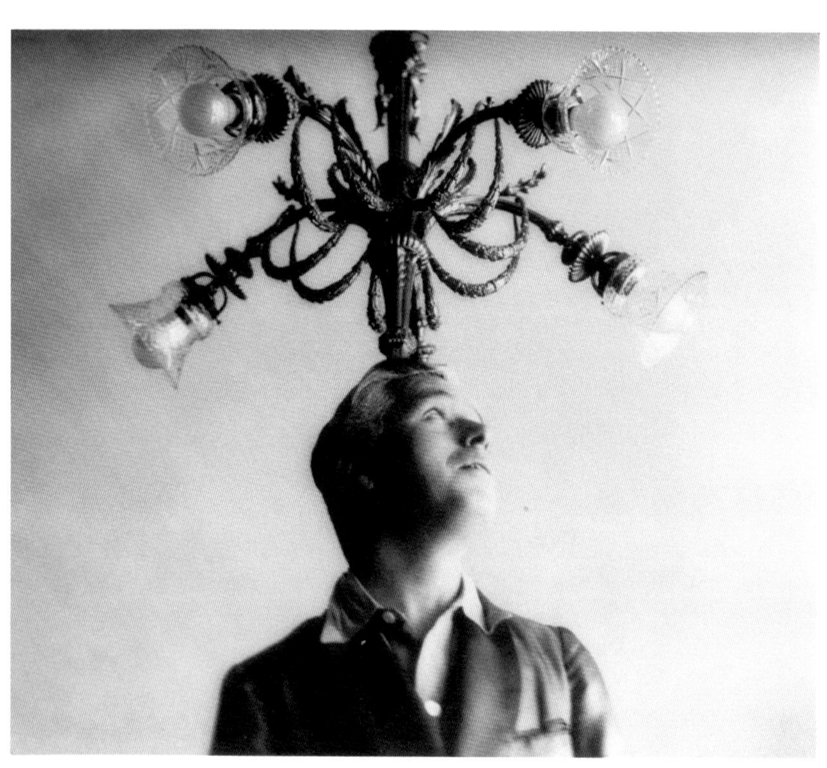

23 **Charlie Chaplin with light fixture**, St Moritz, Switzerland 1932

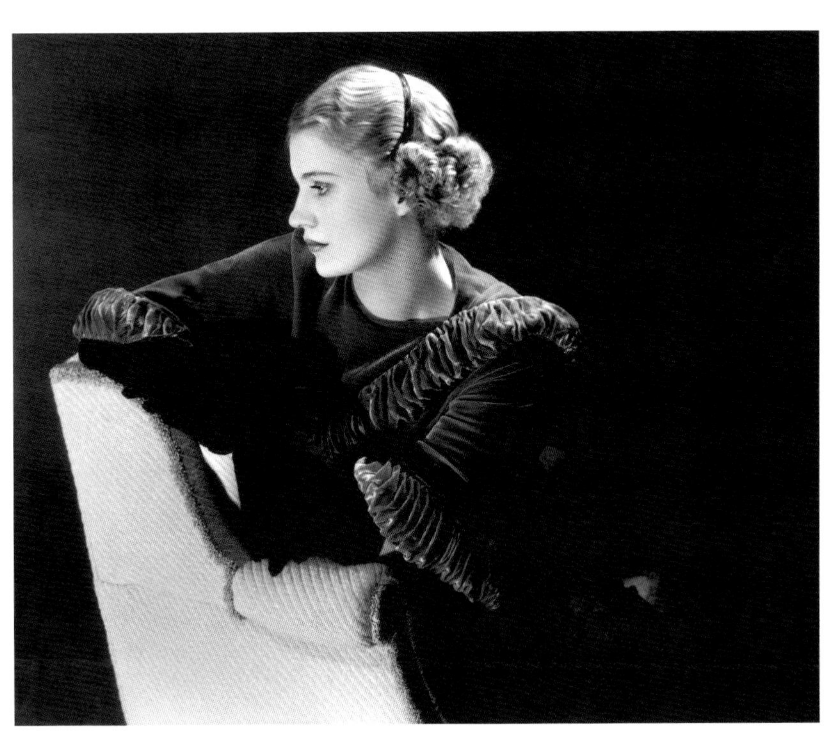

24 **Self-portrait with headband**, New York, USA c1932

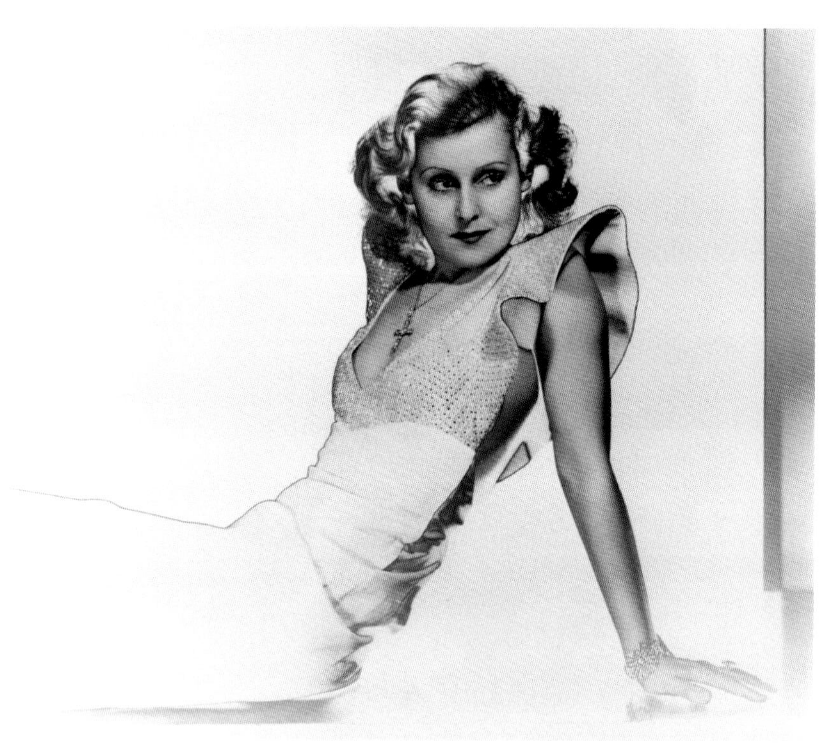

25 **Lilian Harvey, solarised portrait**, New York, USA 1933

26 **Dorothy Hill**, New York, USA 1933

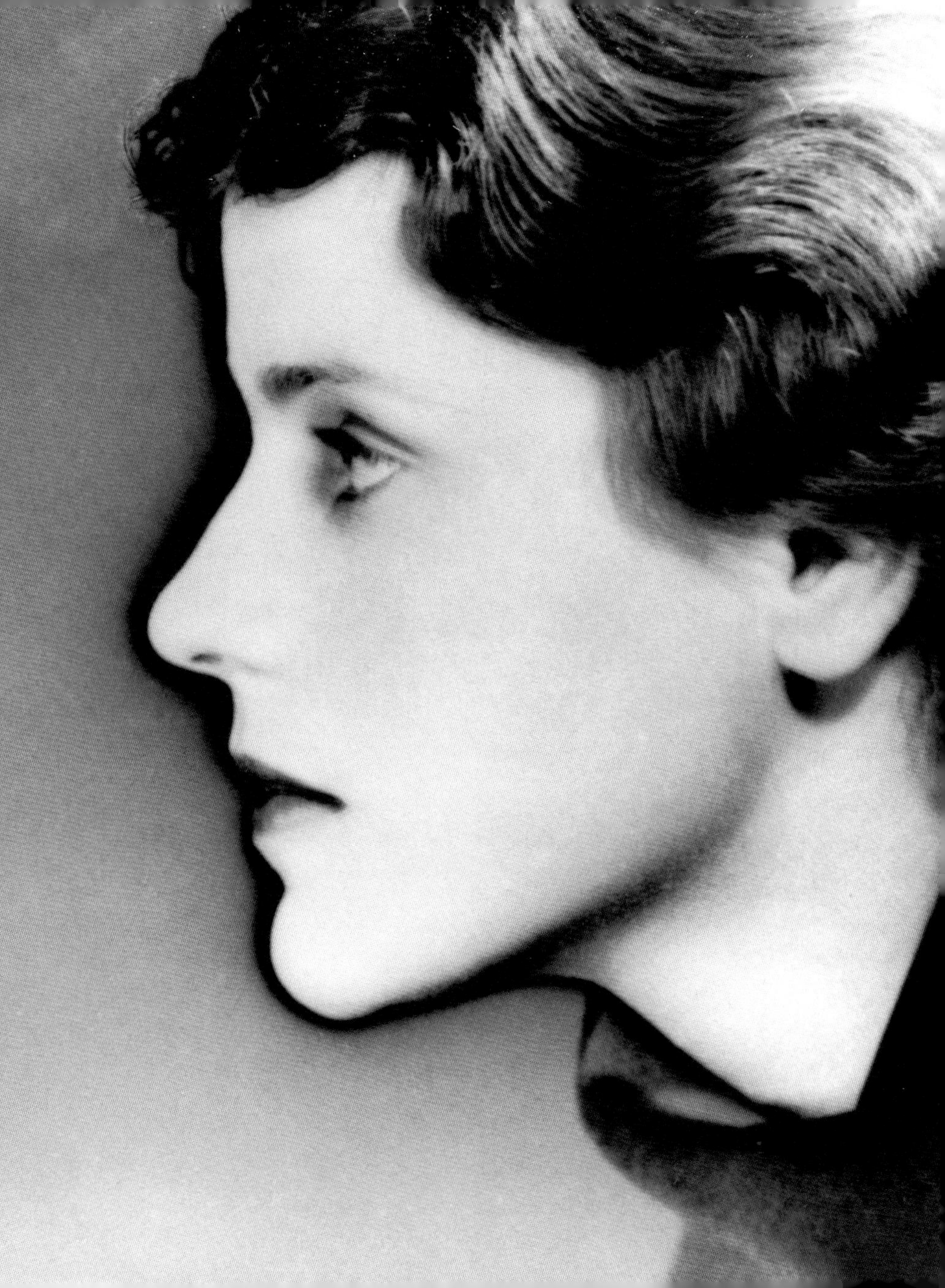

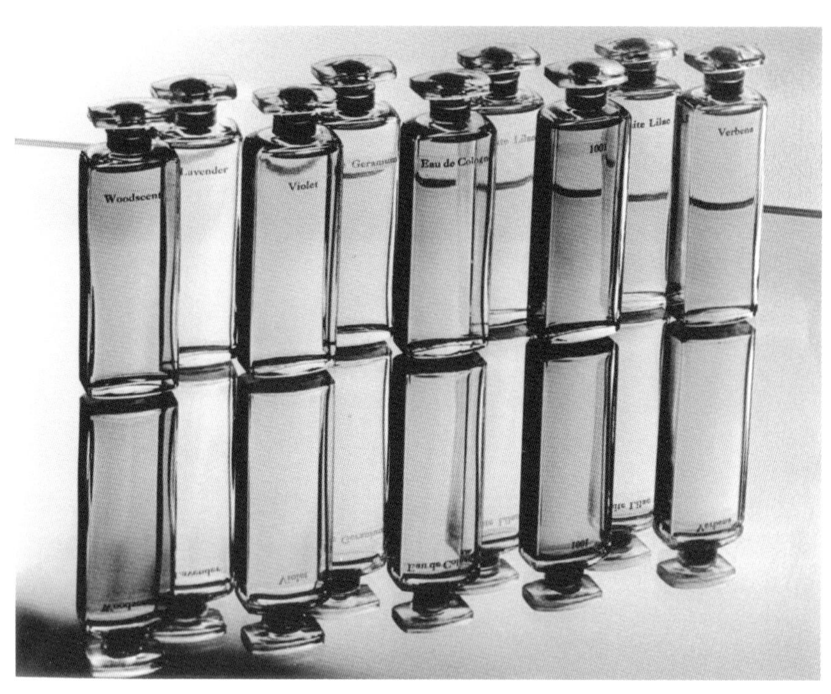

27 **Scent Bottles**, New York, USA 1933

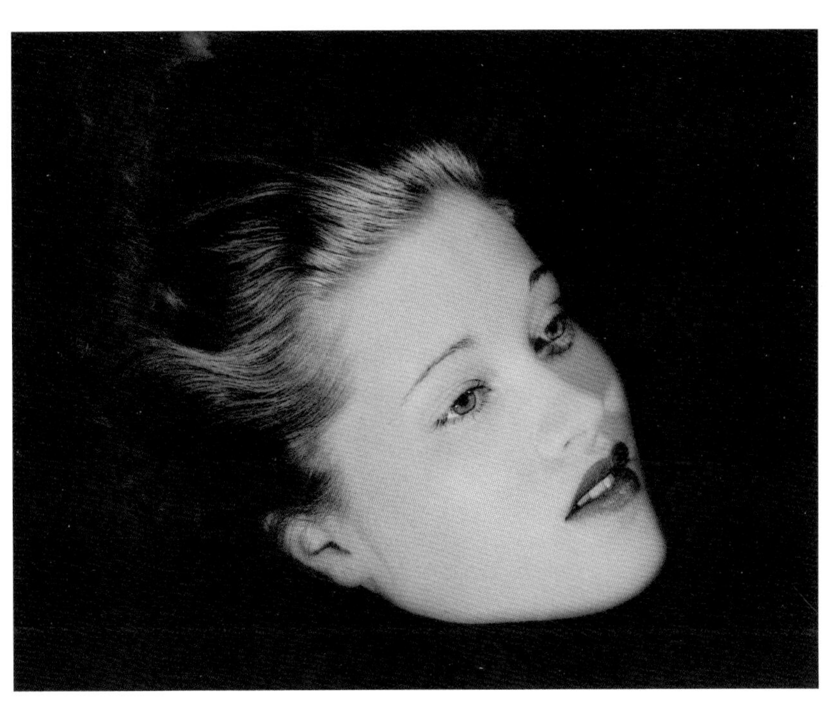

28 **Floating Head, Mary Taylor**, New York, USA 1933

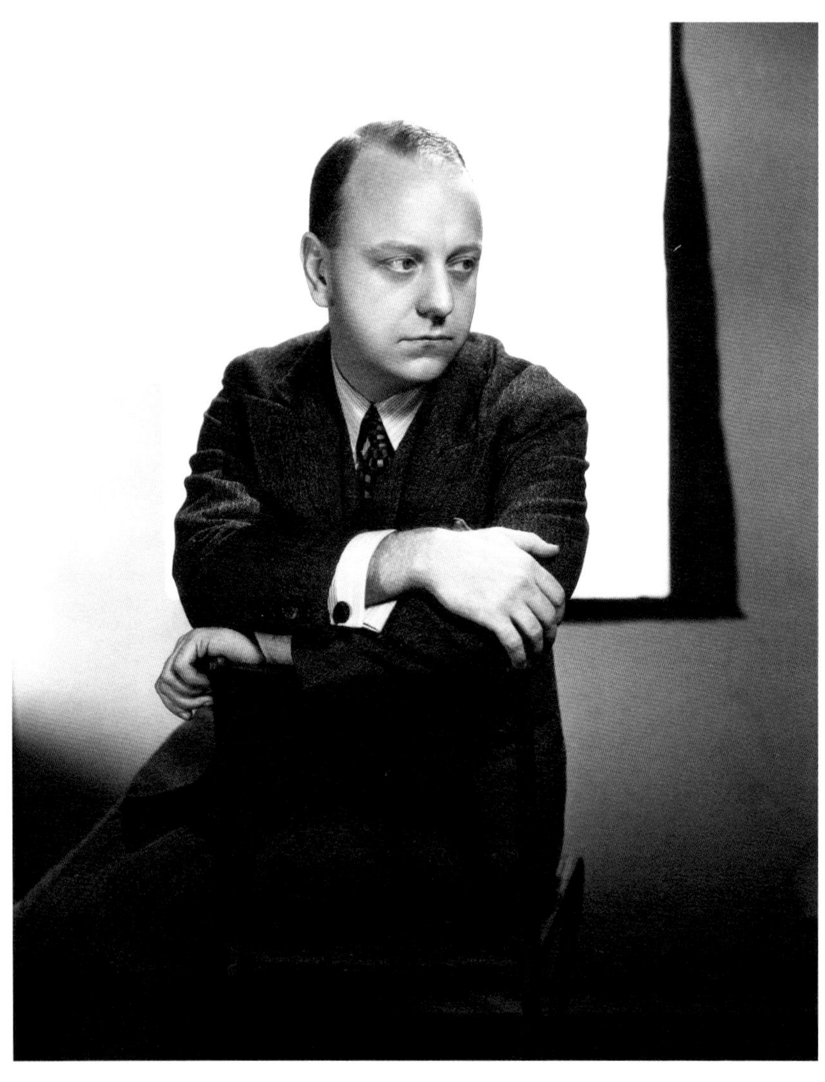

29 **Virgil Thomson, Composer**, New York, USA c1933

30 **Joseph Cornell**, New York, USA 1933

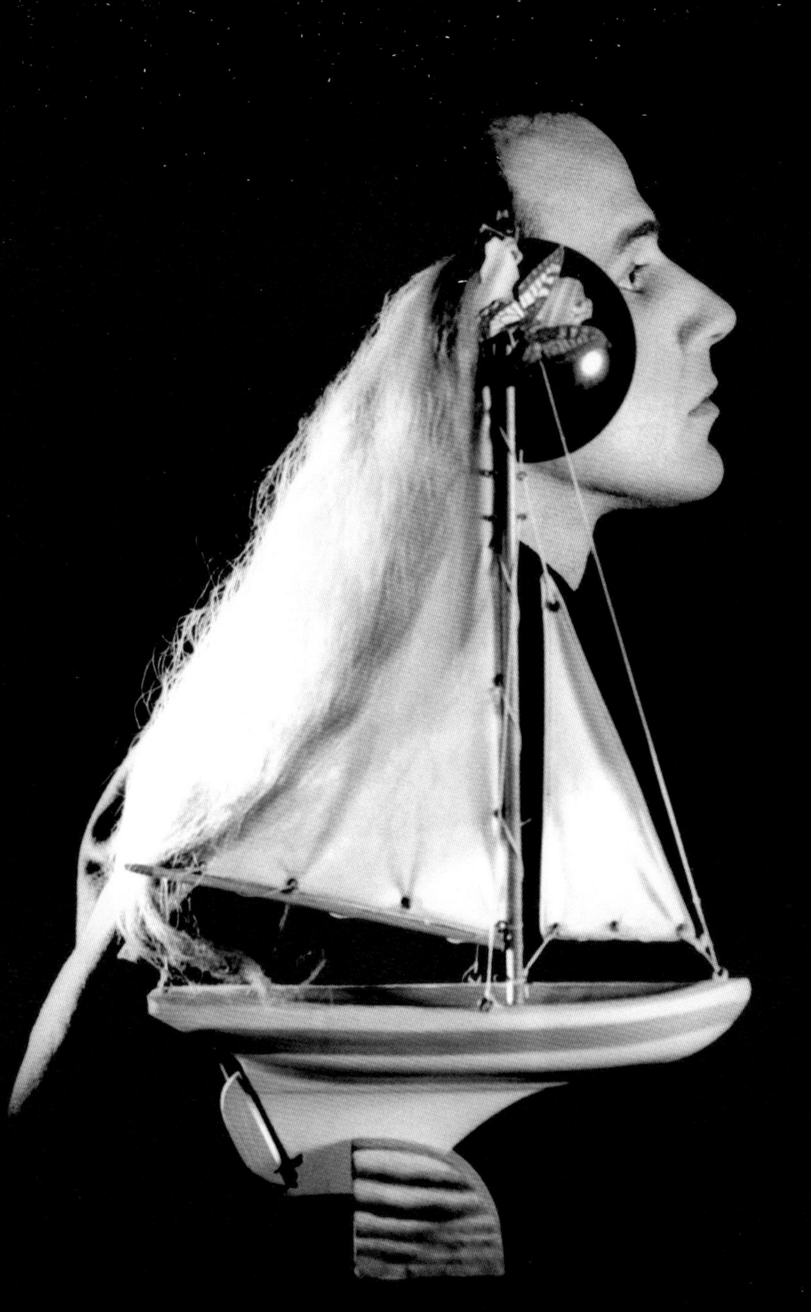

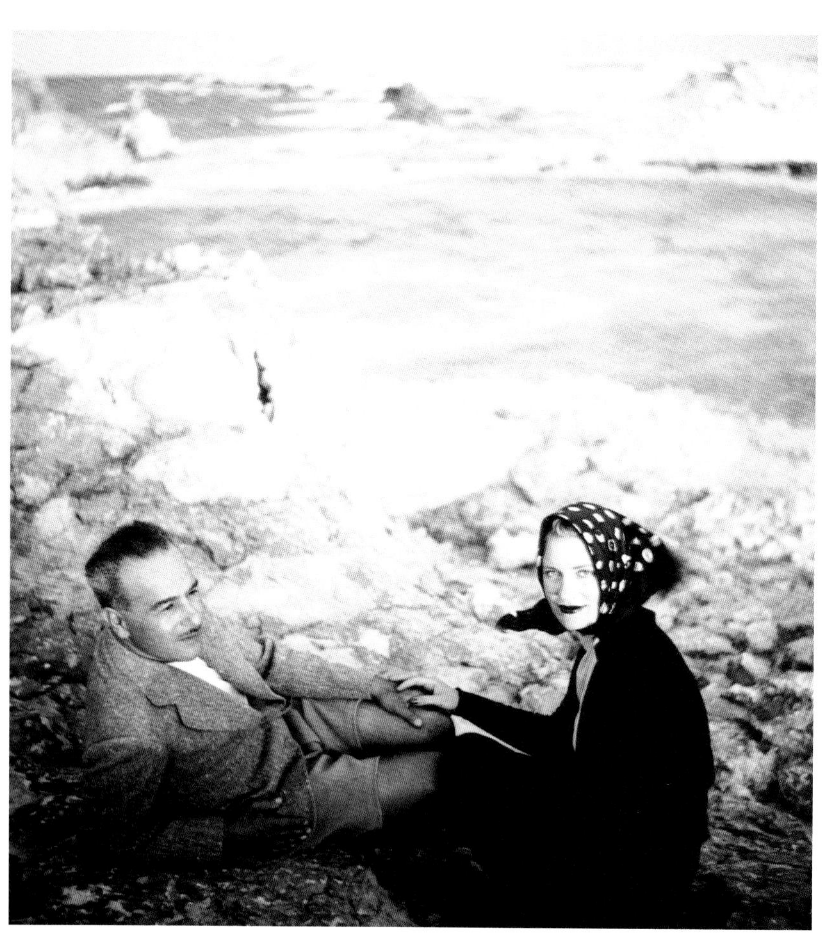

31 **Aziz Eloui Bey and Lee Miller,** Egypt c1935

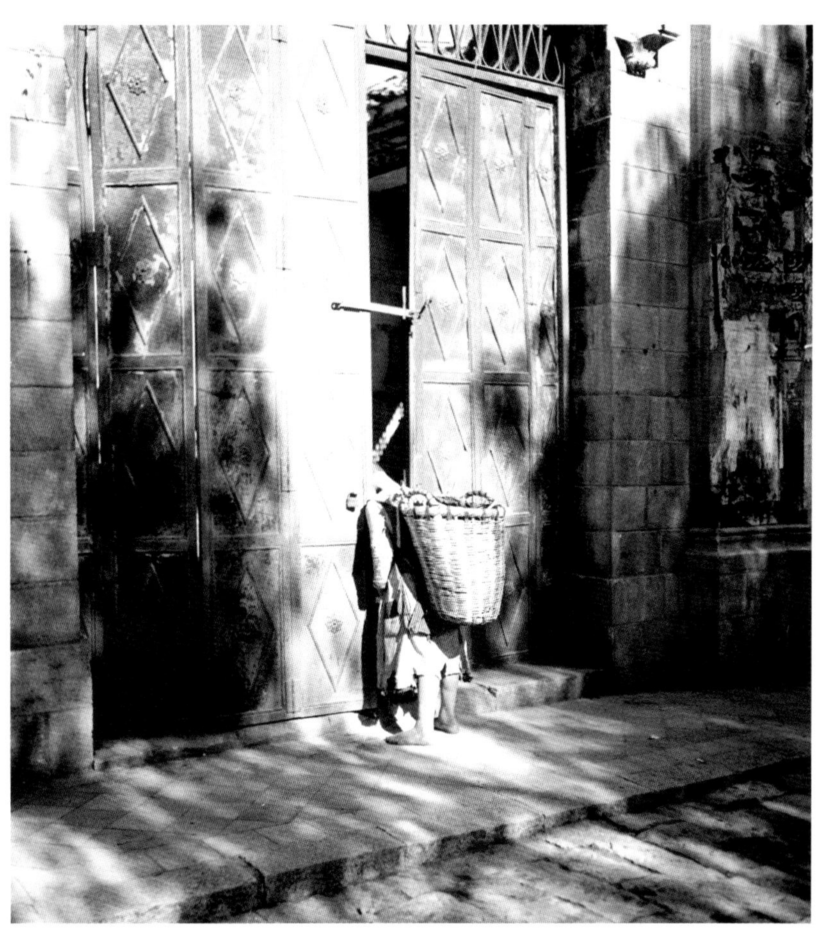

32 **Untitled [Man with basket in doorway]**, Egypt c1936

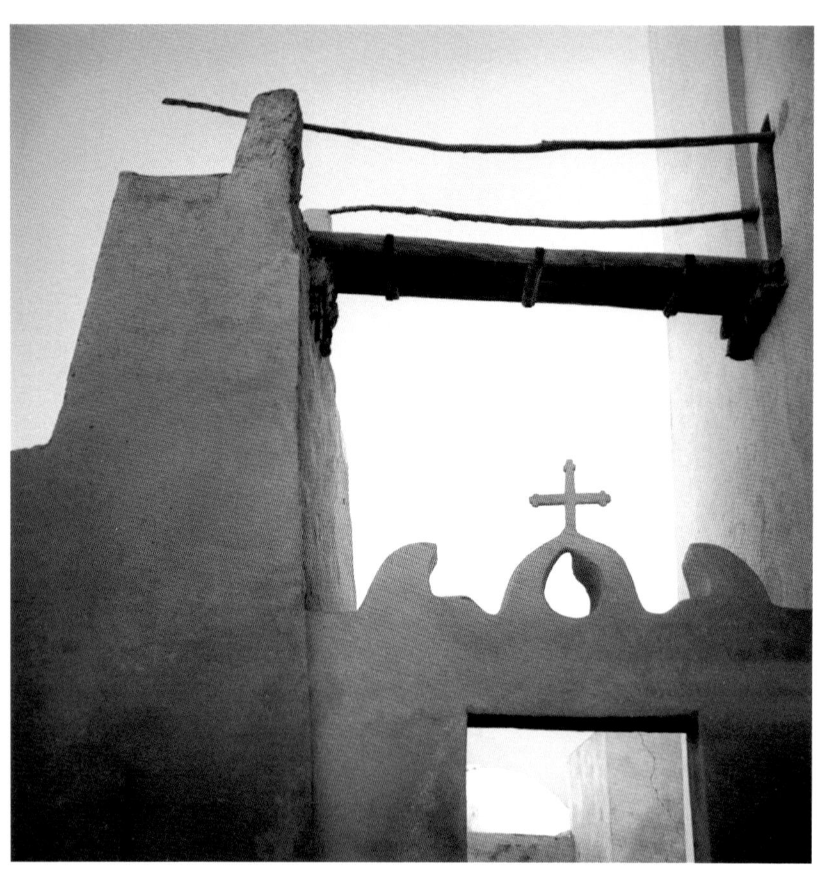

33 **The Drawbridge of Deir El Soriani Monastery,** Wadi Natrun, Egypt c1936

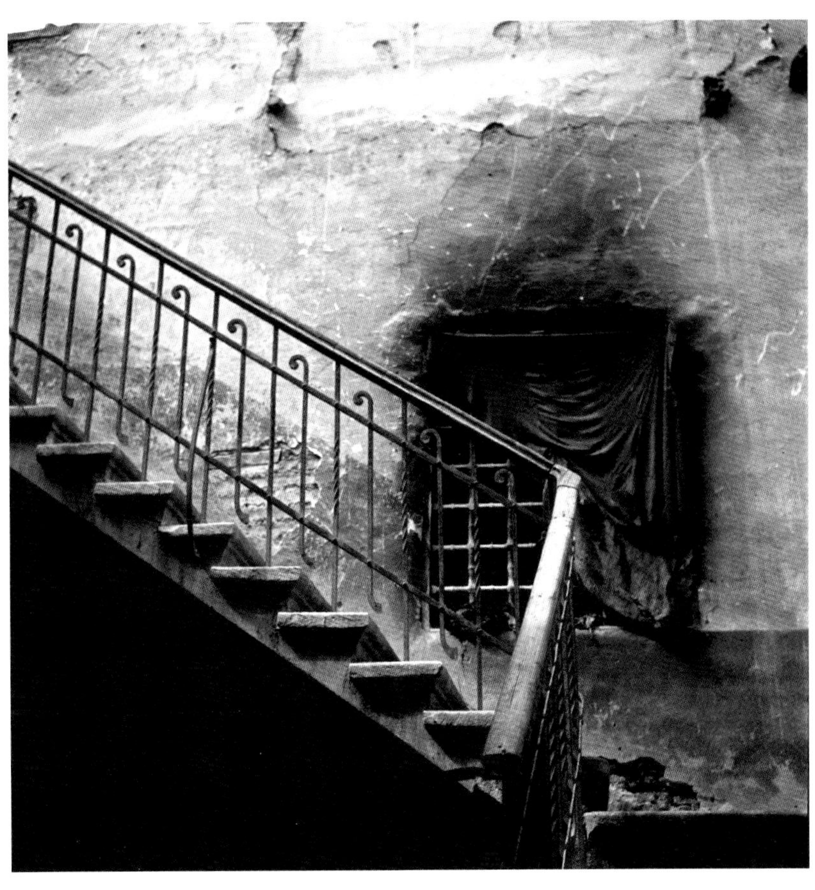

34 **Untitled [Stairway]**, Cairo, Egypt c1936

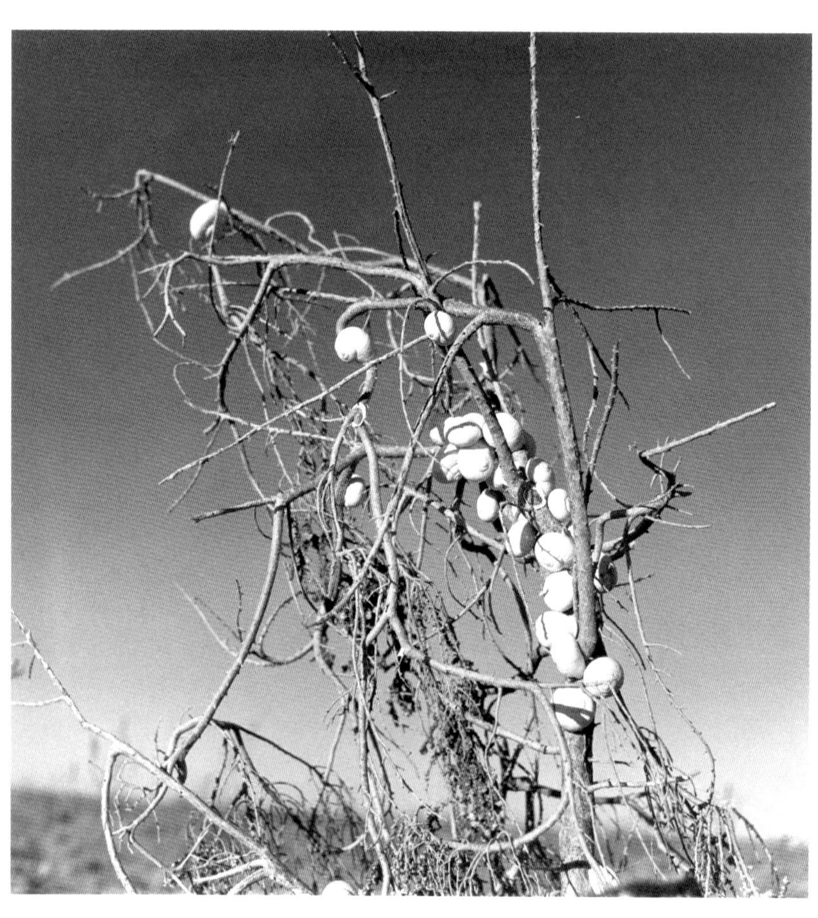

35 **Untitled [Bleached snail shells]**, Western Desert, Egypt c1936

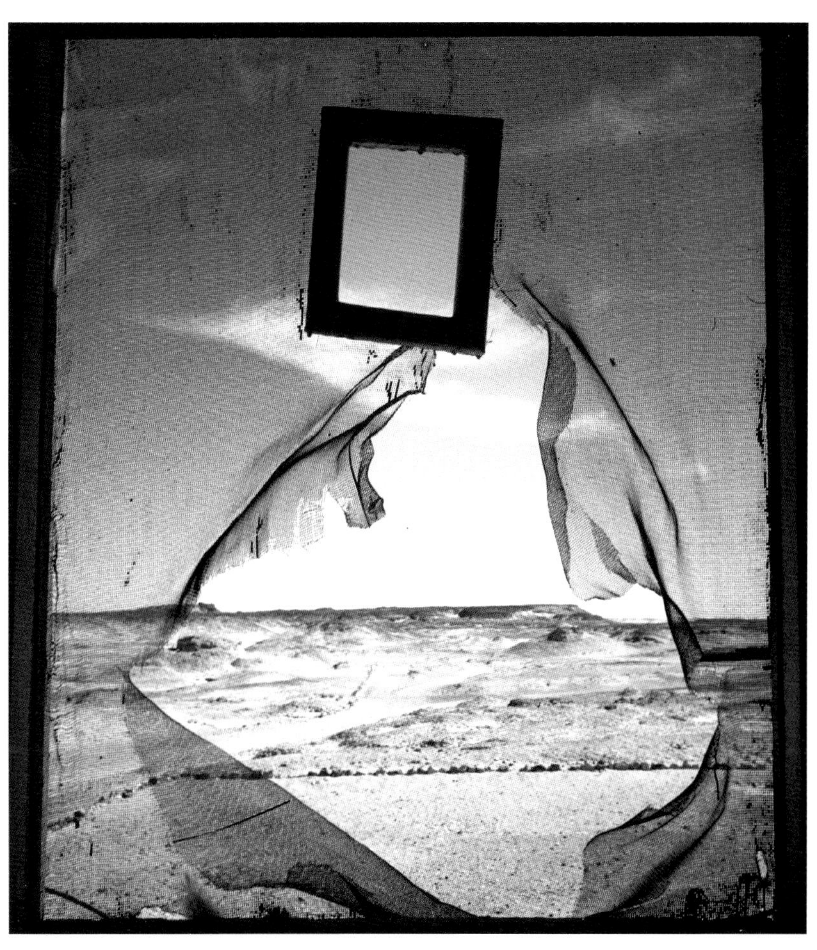

36 **Portrait of Space**, Near Siwa, Egypt 1937

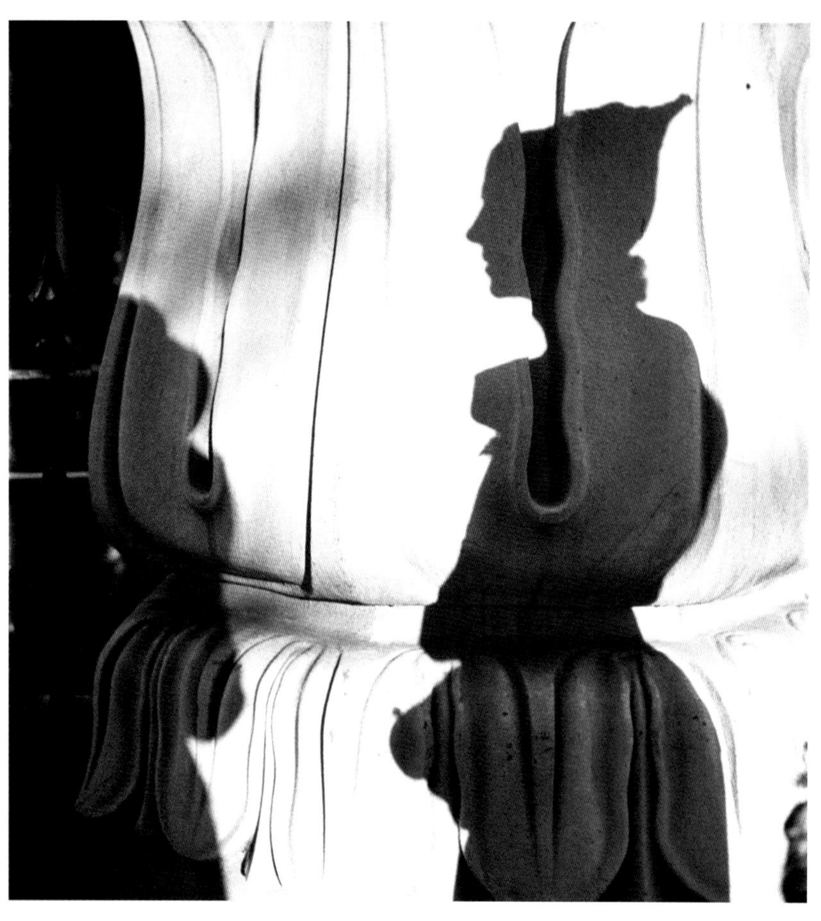

37 **Eileen Agar at the Royal Pavilion**, Brighton, England 1937

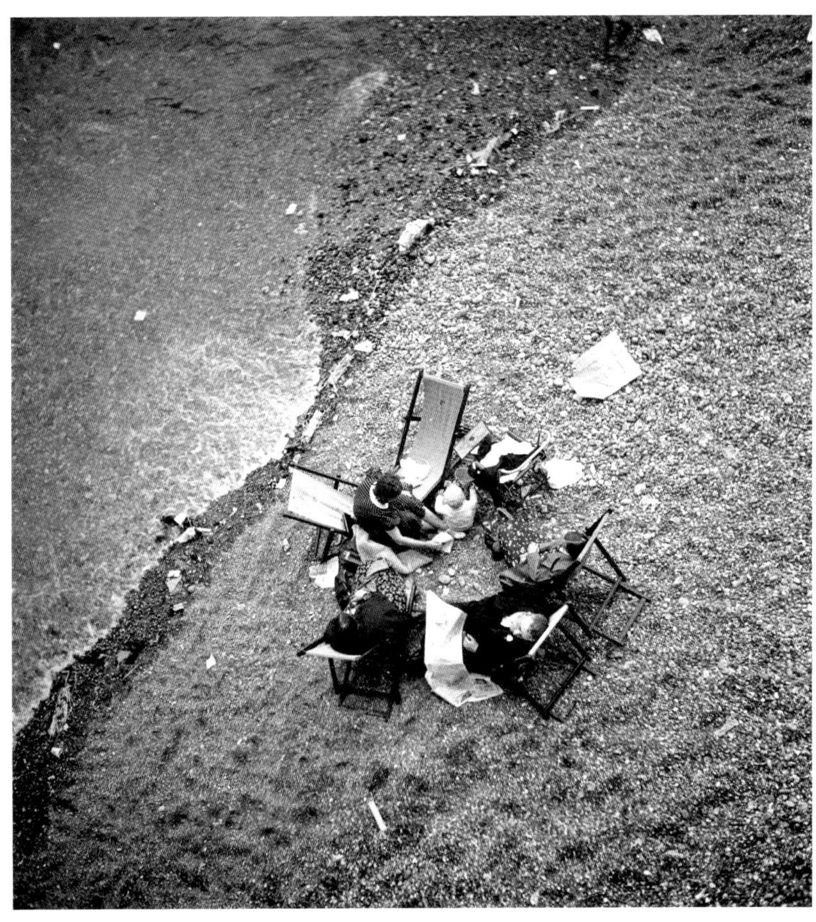

38 **Brighton Beach**, East Sussex, England 1937

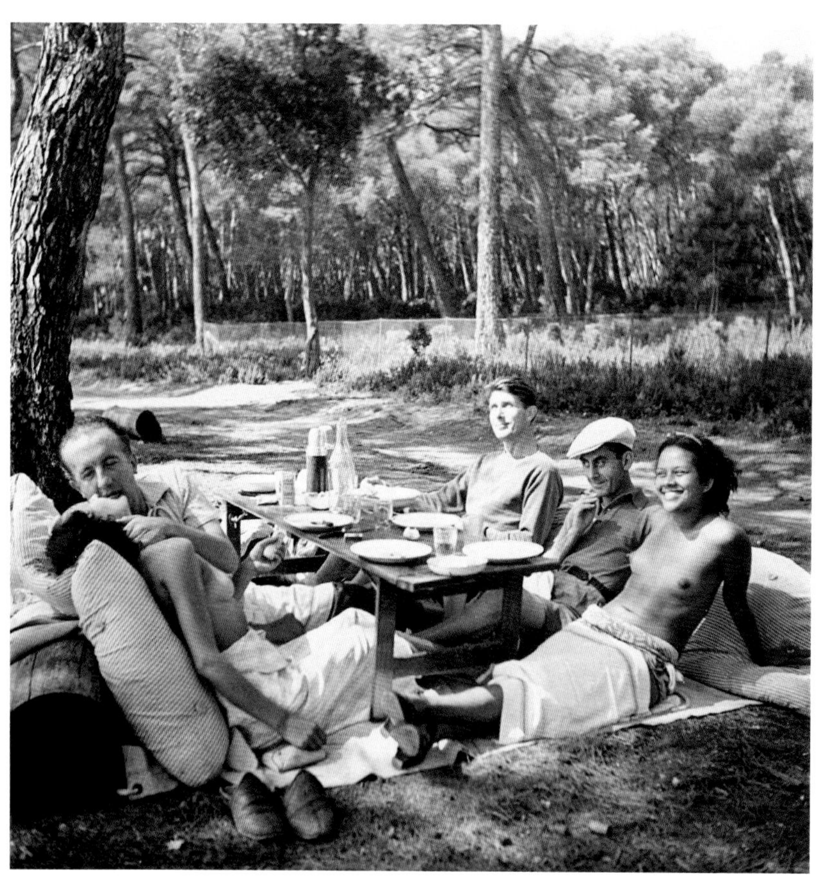

39 **Picnic**, Ile Sainte Marguerite, France 1937

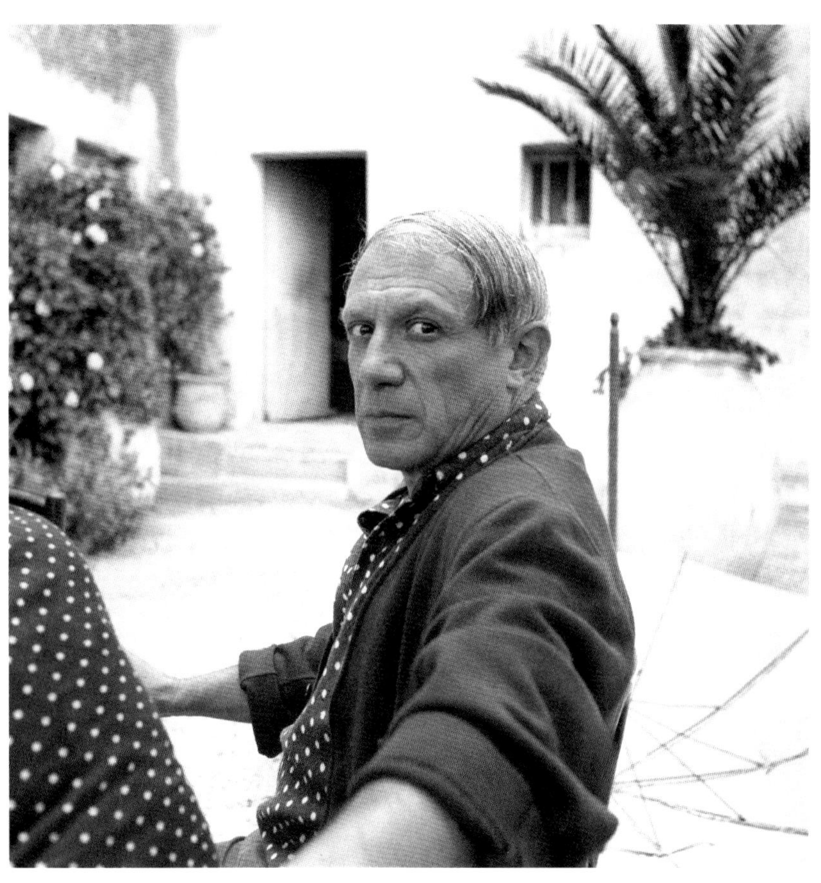

40 **Picasso**, Mougins, France 1937

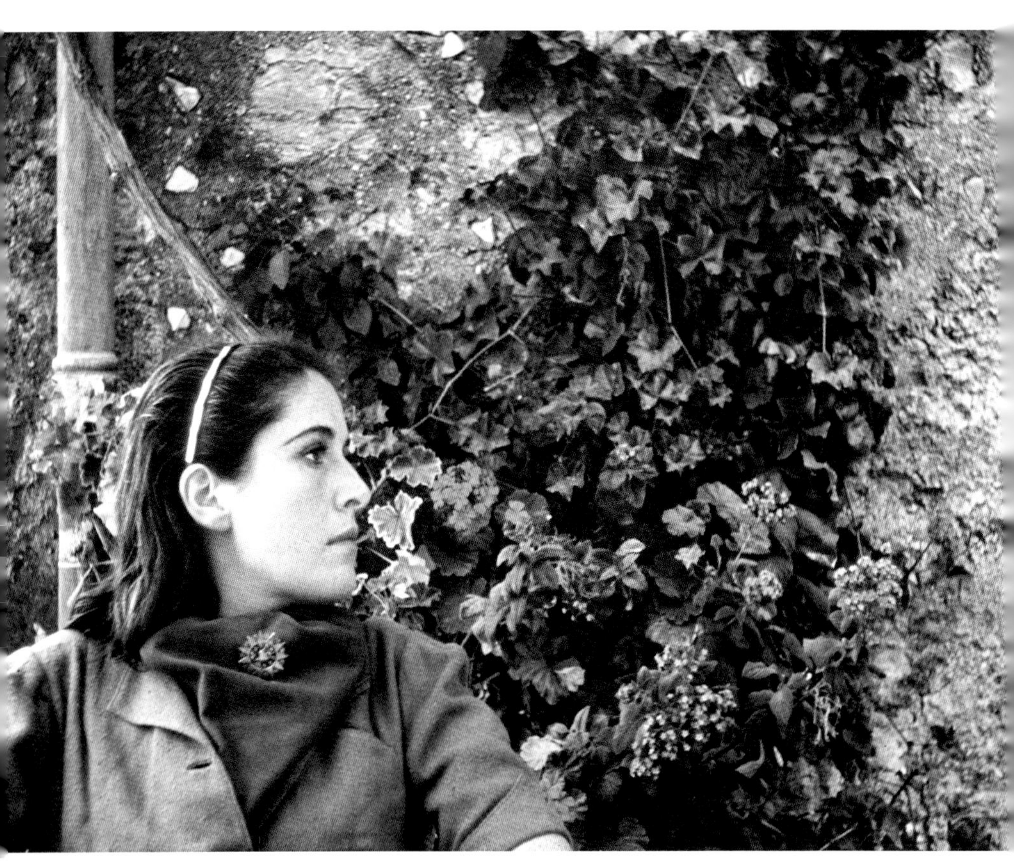

41 **Dora Maar**, Mougins, France 1937

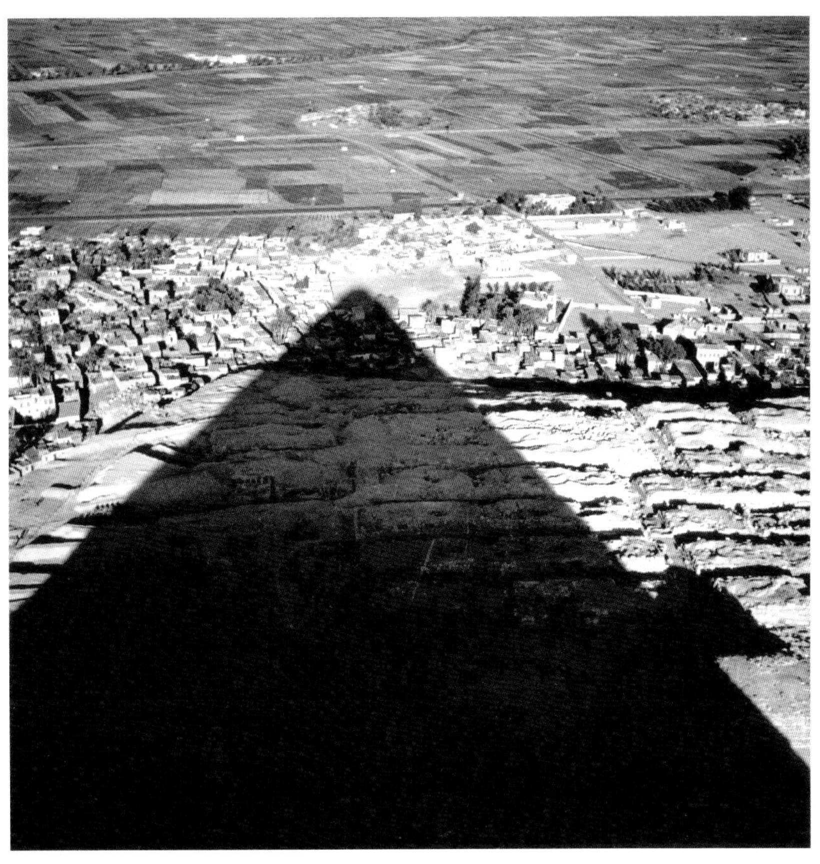

42 **From the top of the Great Pyramid**, Giza, Egypt c1937

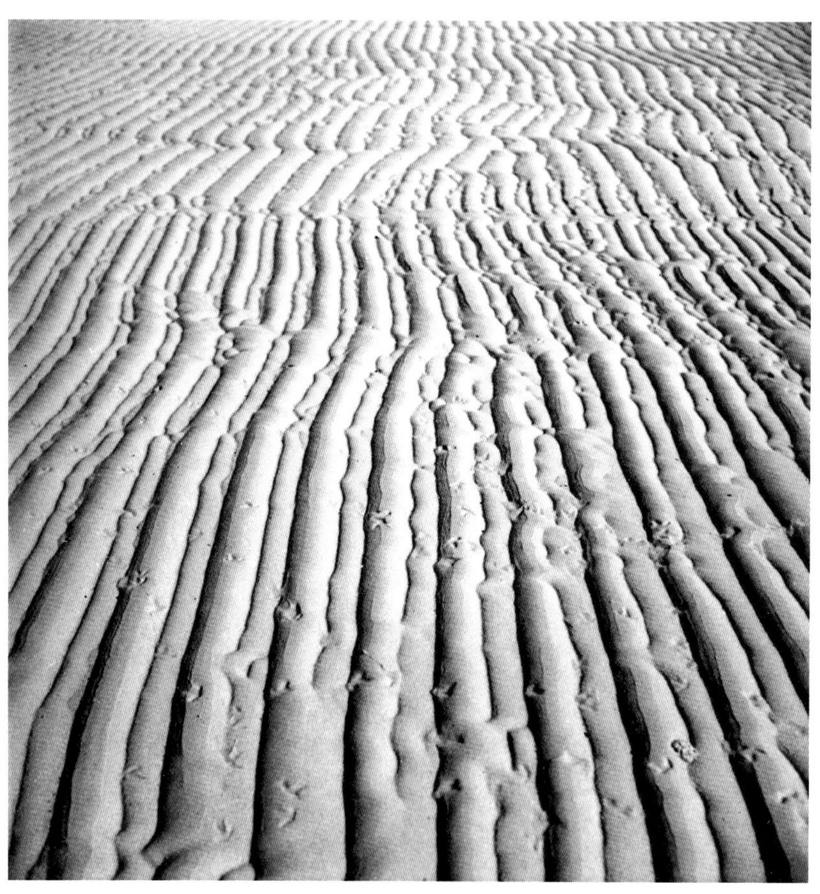

43 **The Procession [Bird Tracks in Sand]**, Ain Sukhana, Egypt c1937

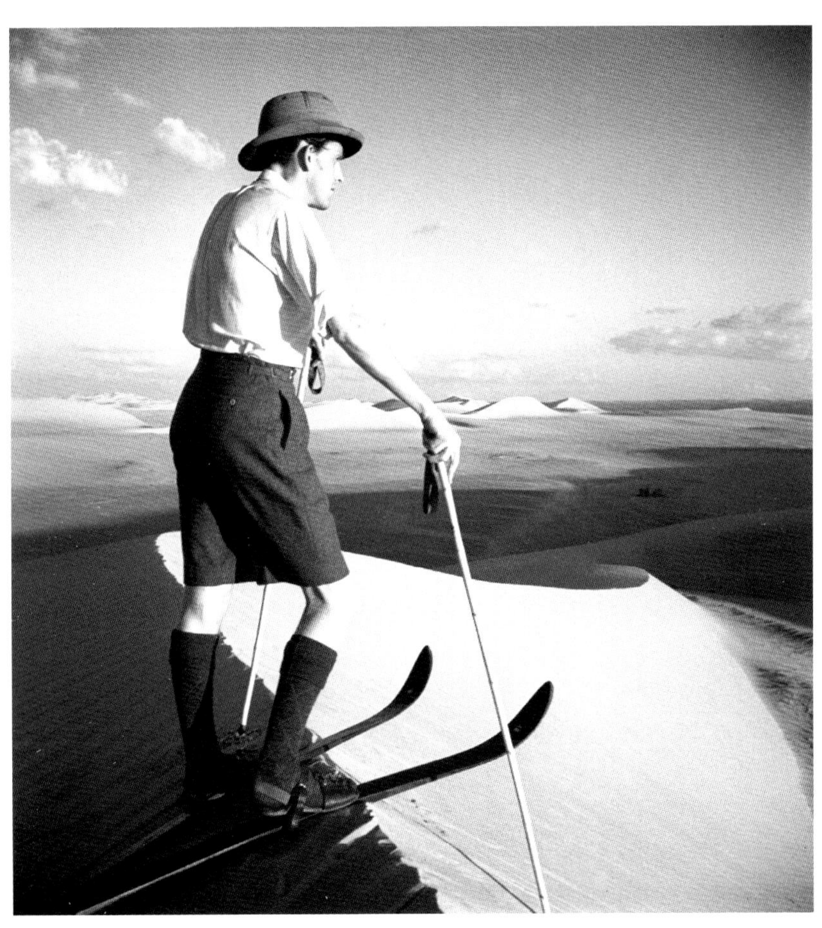

44 **Robin Fedden**, Egypt 1937

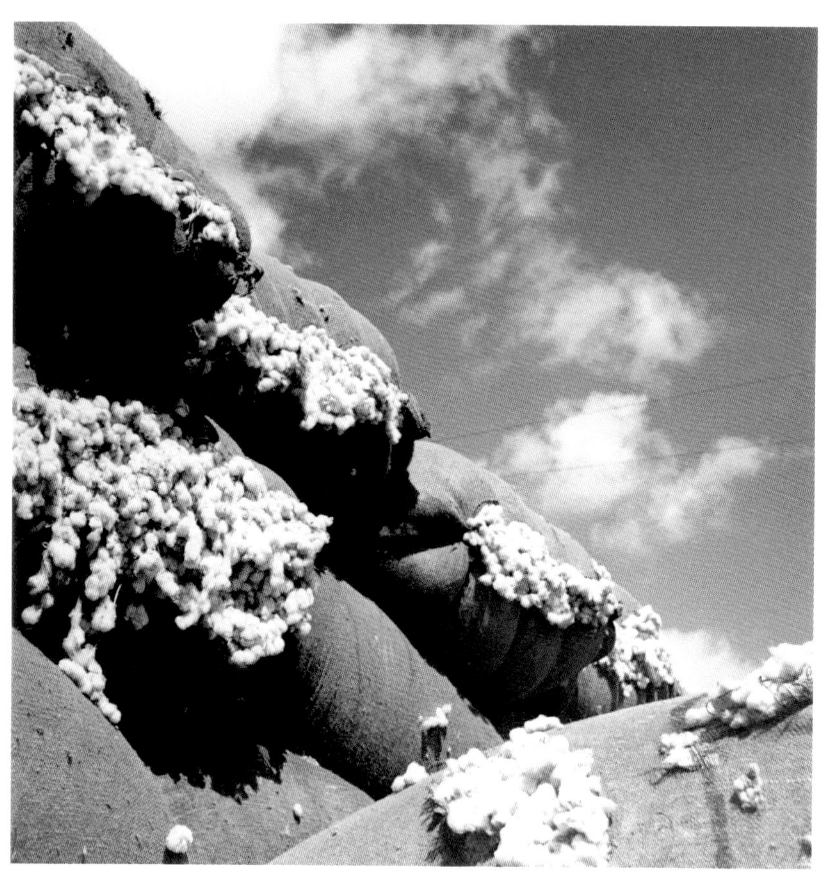

45 **Untitled [Cotton Sacks]**, Assyut, Egypt 1939

46 **Untitled [Legs: Mafy Miller, unknown, George Hoyningen-Heuné and Roland Penrose]**, Gebel Mawta, Siwa, Egypt 1939

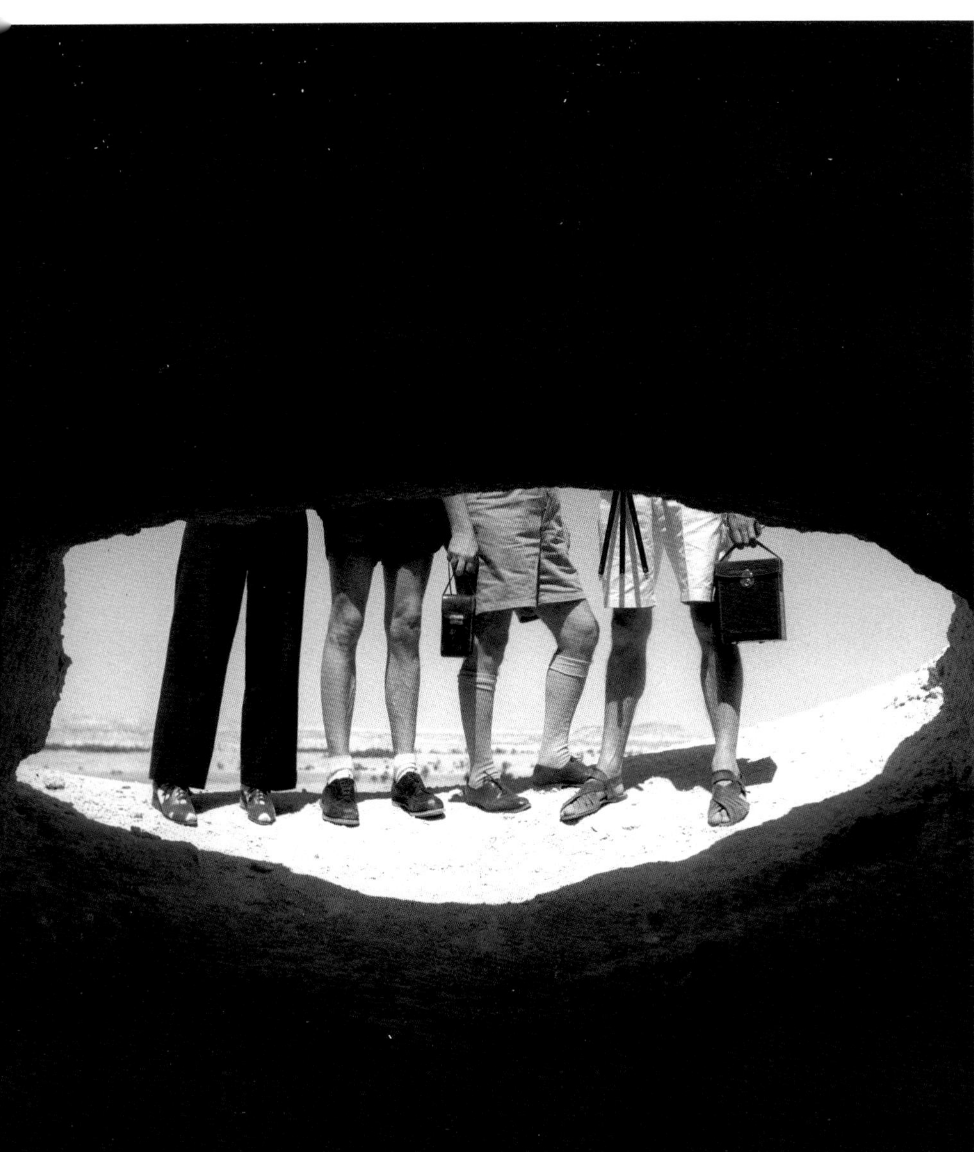

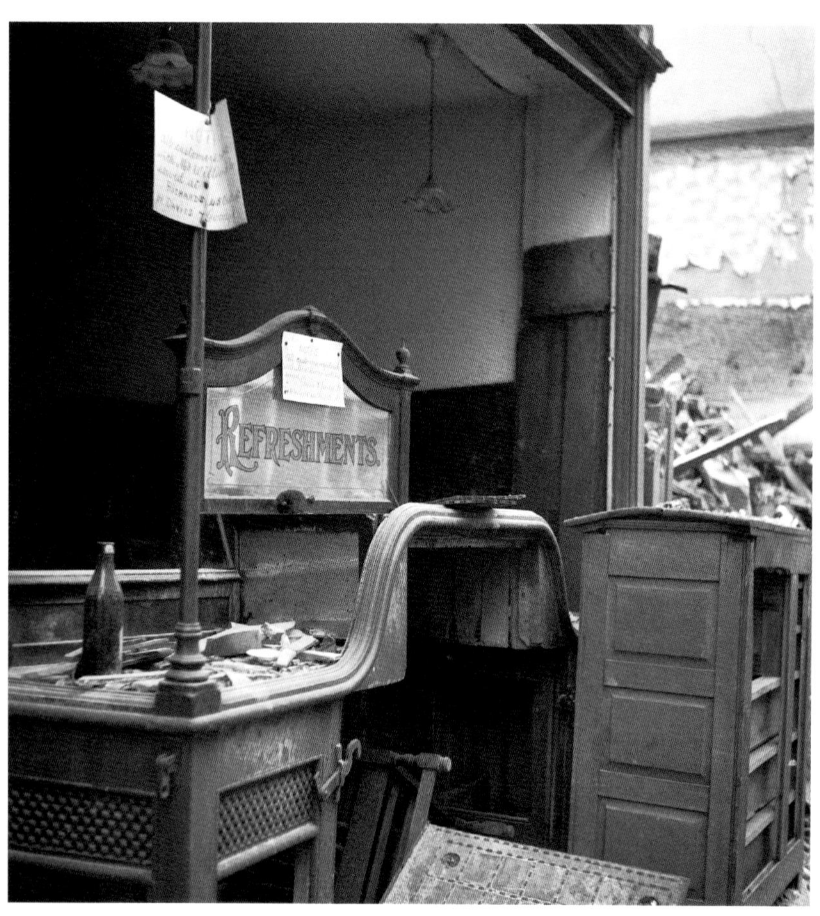

47 **Tea will be a little late today**, London, England 1940

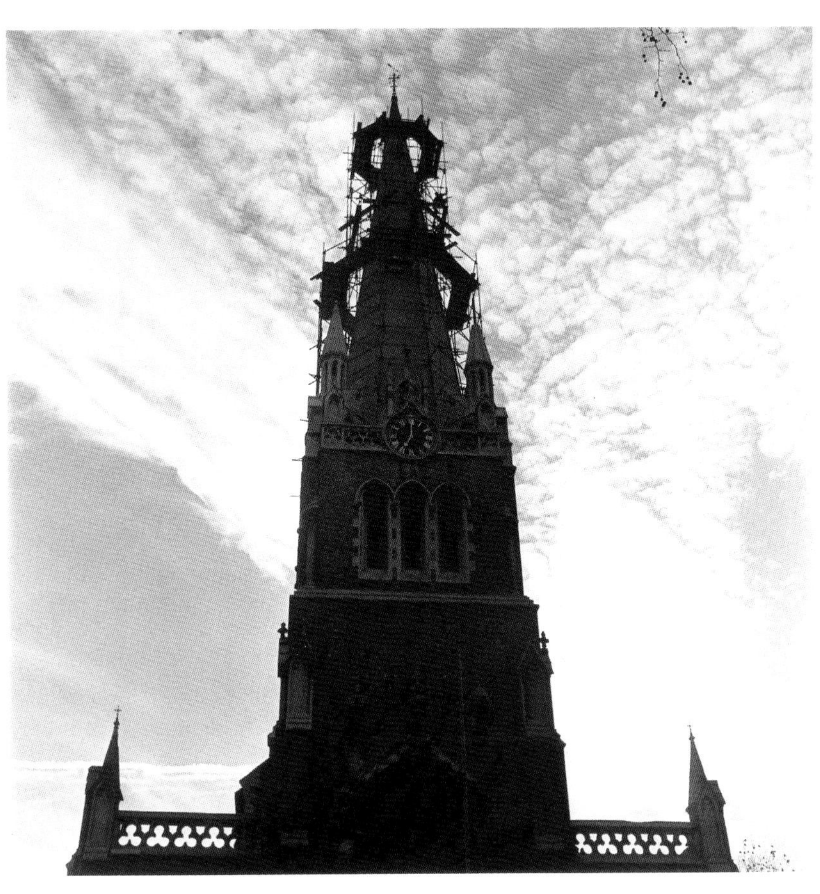

48 **St James**, London, England 1940

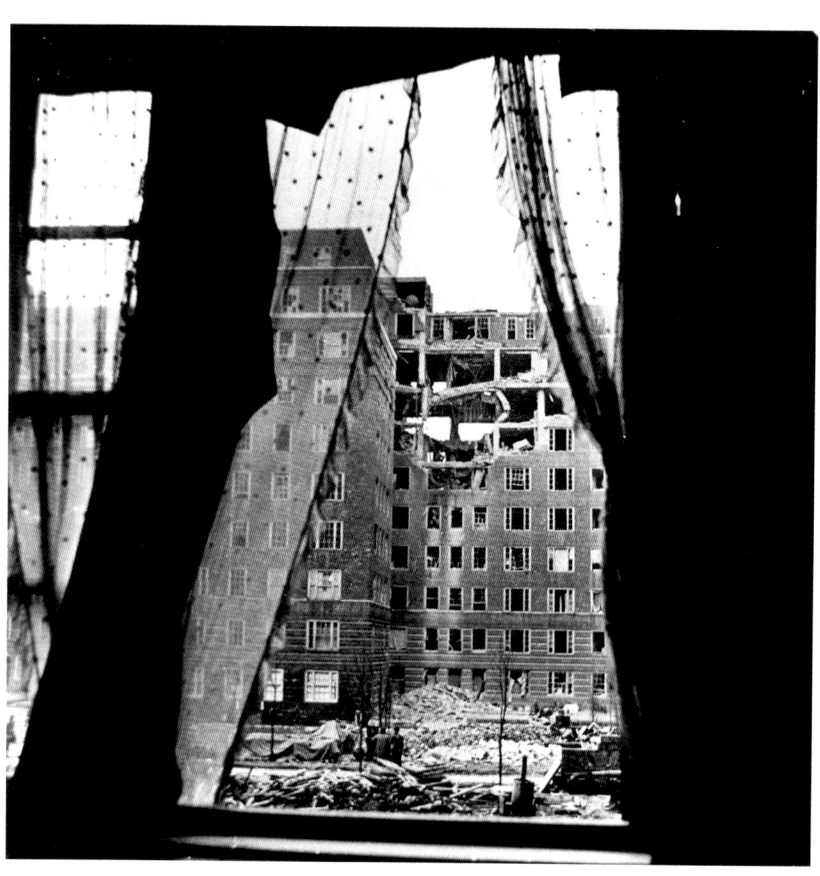

49 **Dolphin Square**, London, England 1940

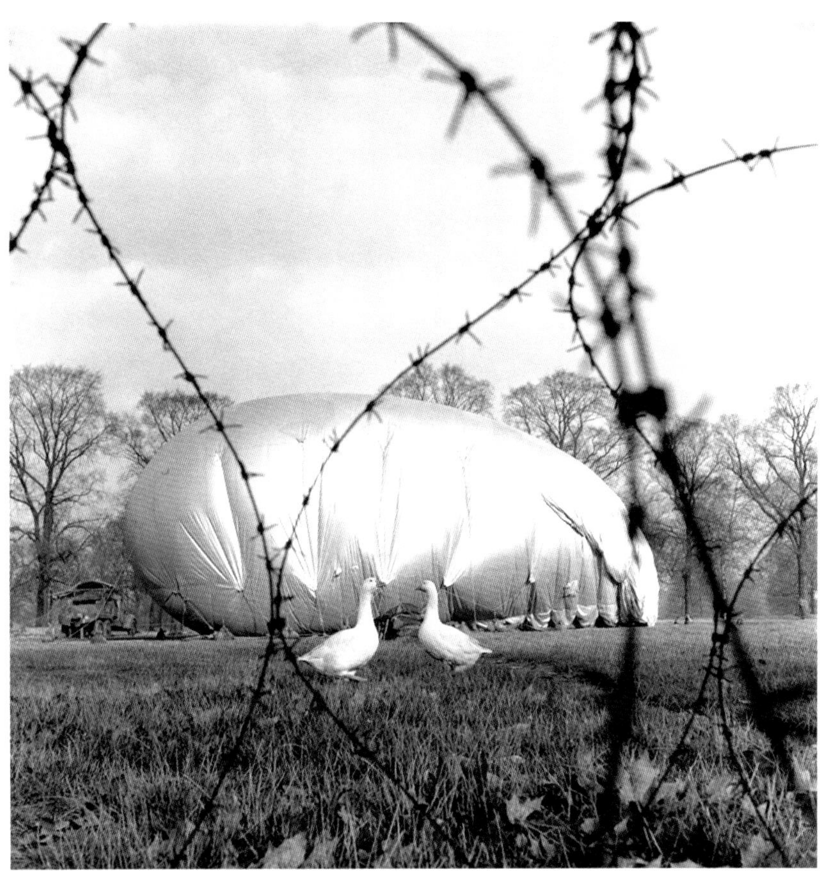

50 **Eggceptional Achievement**, London, England 1940

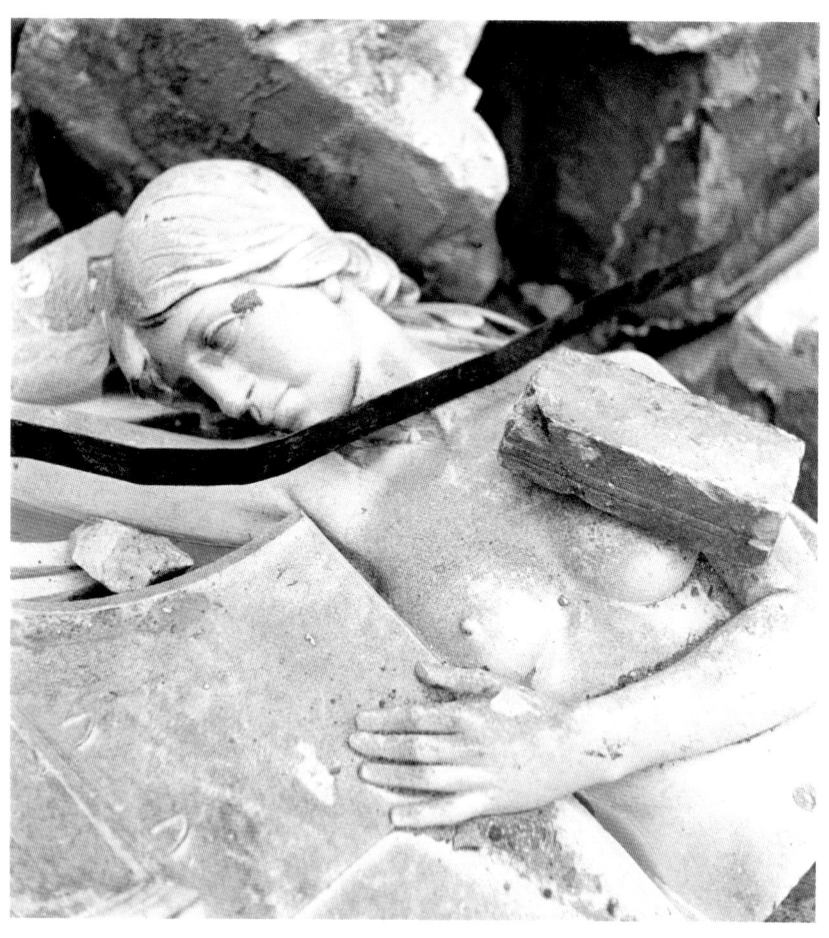

51 **Revenge on Culture**, London, England 1940

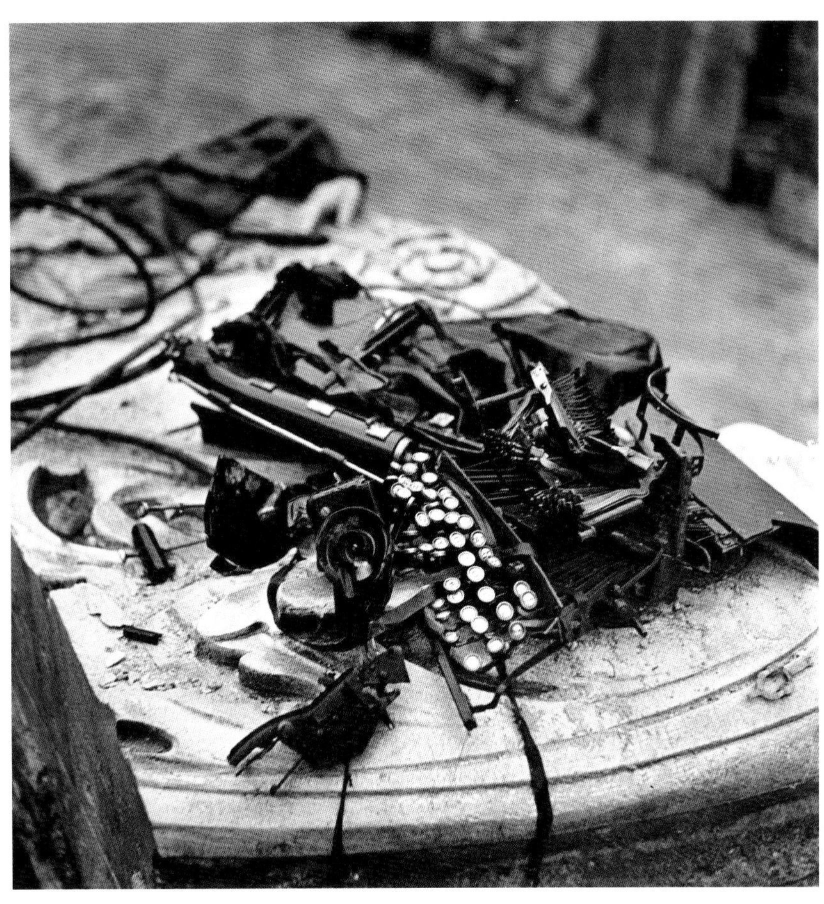

52 **Remington Silent**, London, England 1940

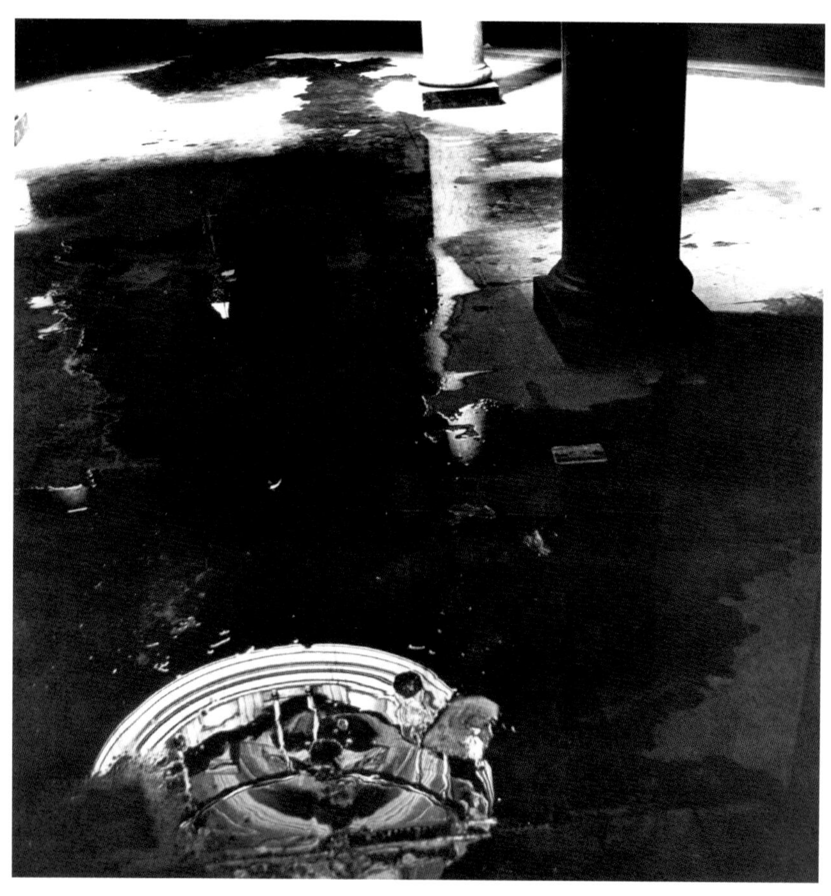

53 **Shattered Roof of University College**, London, England 1940

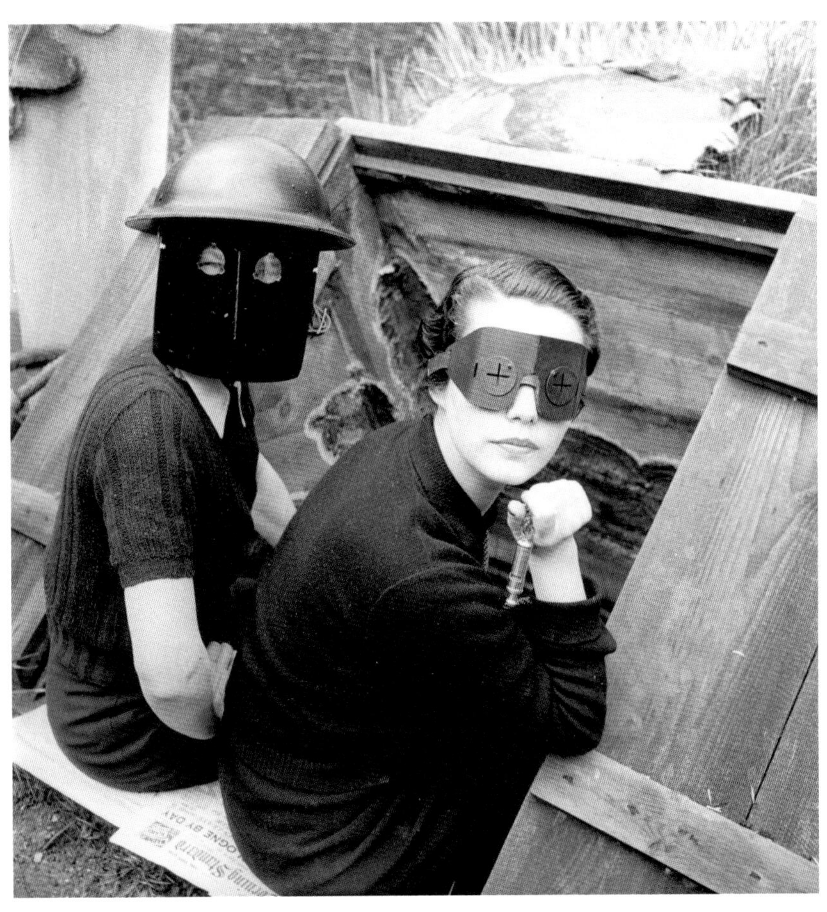

54 **Fire Masks**, London, England 1941

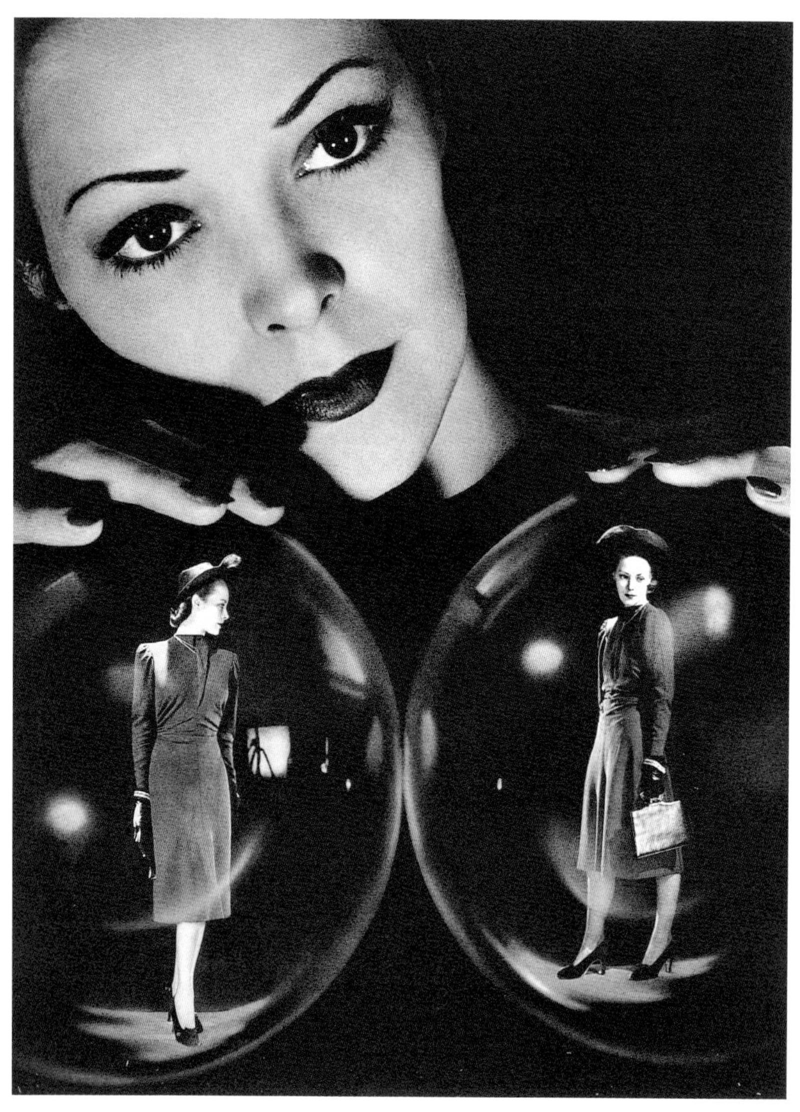

55 **Good and bad posture**, London, England 1942

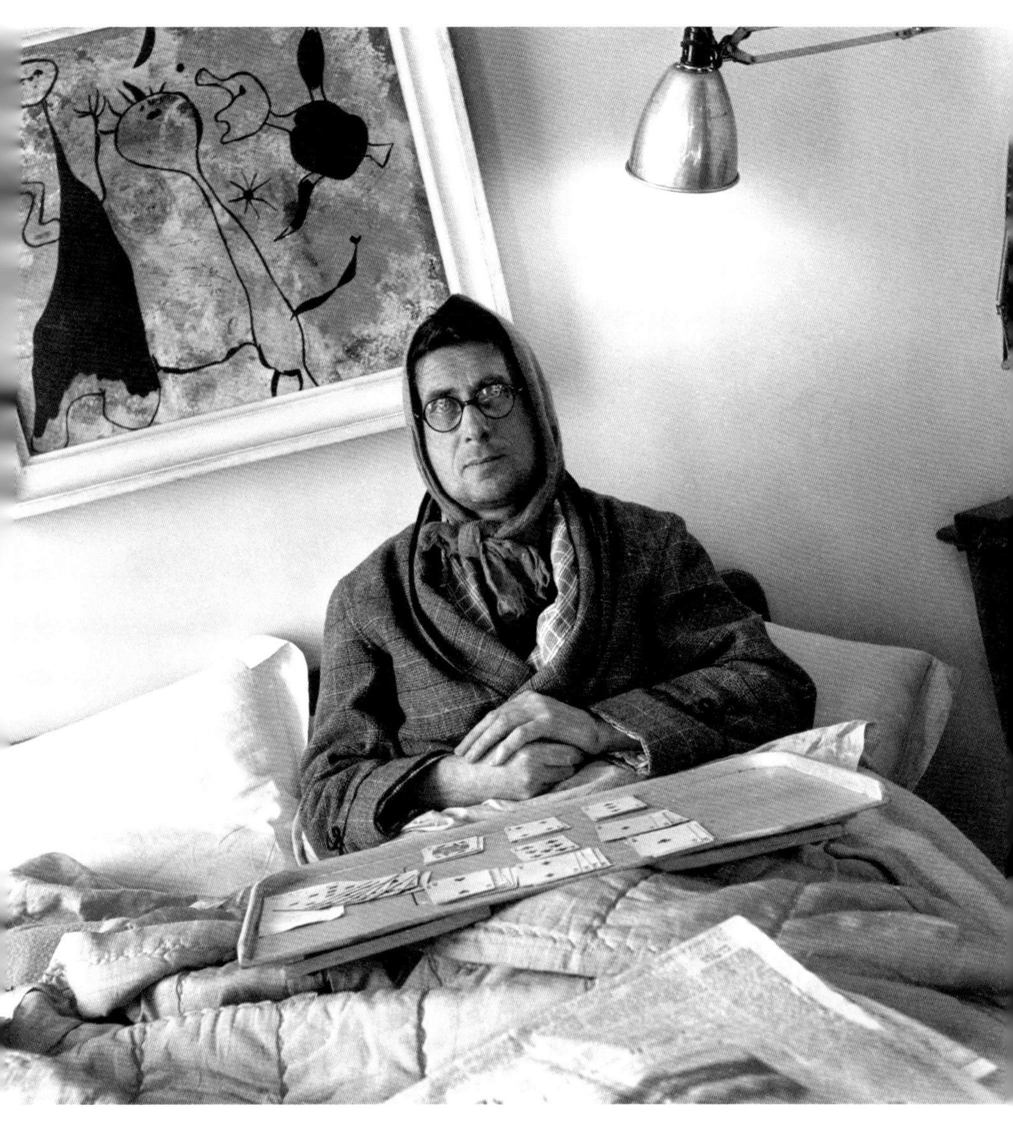

56 **Roland Penrose with mumps**, Downshire Hill, London, England 1942

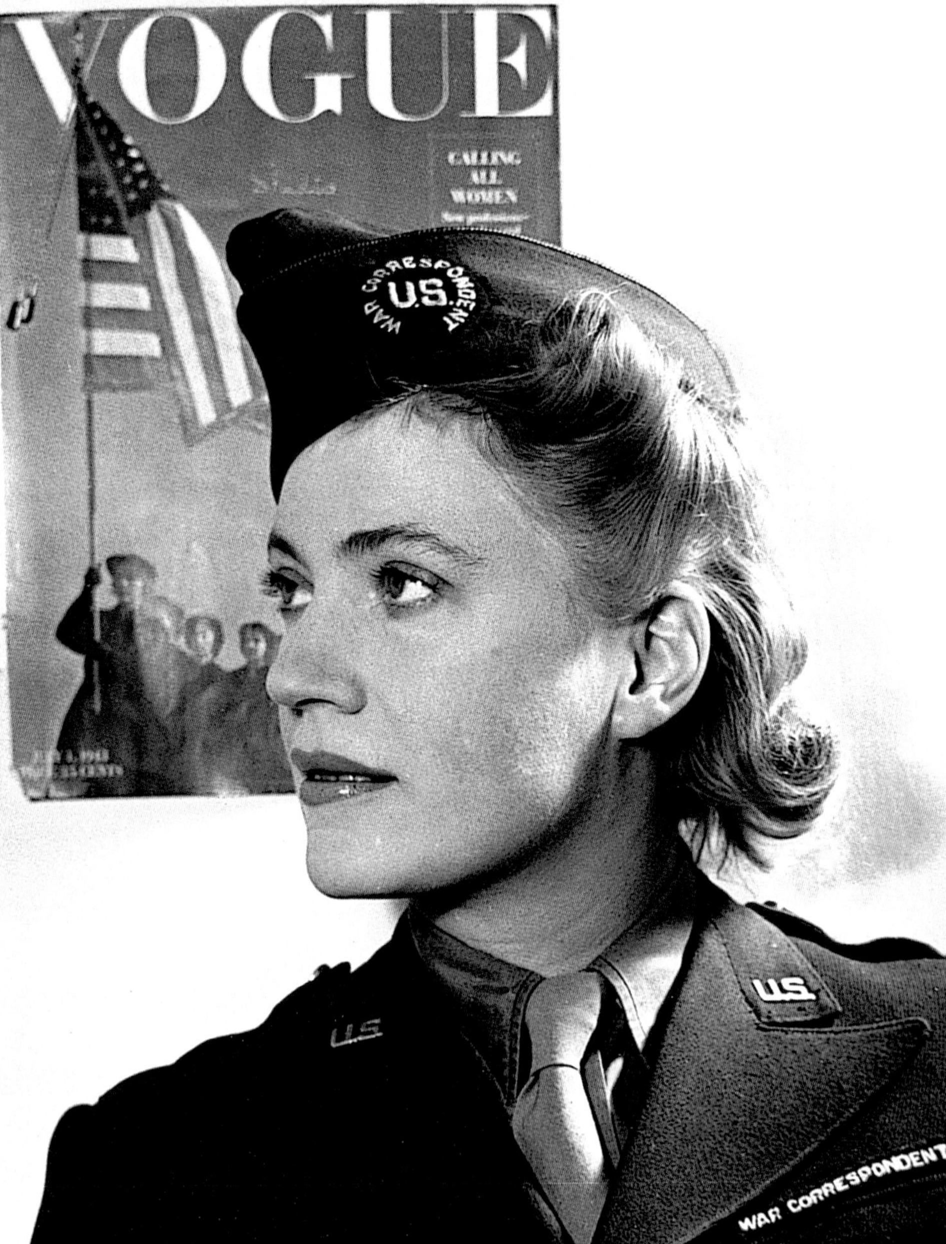
VOGUE
CALLING
ALL
WOMEN
WAR CORRESPONDENT
U.S.
U.S.
U.S.
WAR CORRESPONDENT

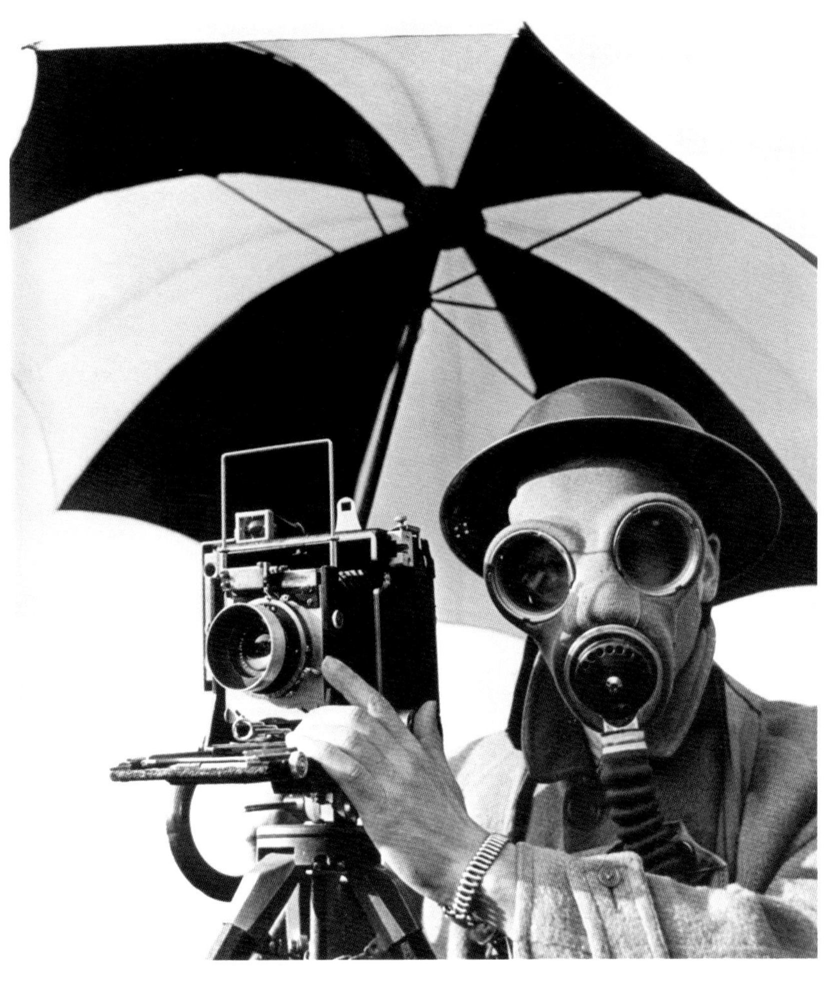

57 **Lee Miller, *Vogue Studio*,** London, England 1943

58 **David E. Scherman, dressed for war,** London, England 1943

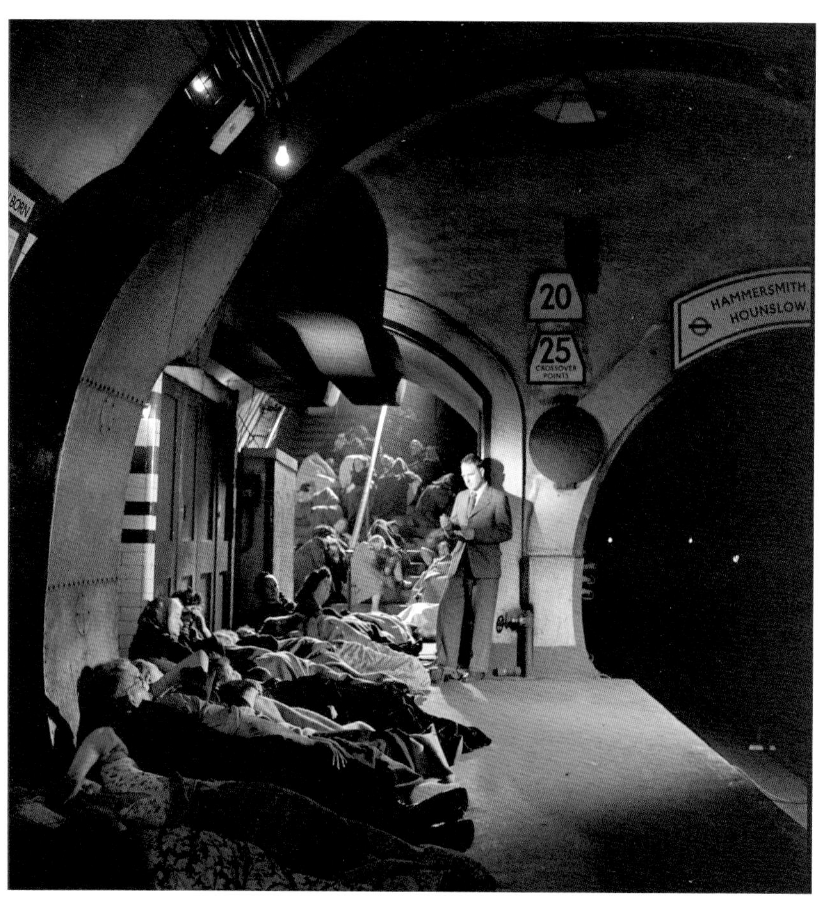

59 **Henry Moore taken during the filming of 'Out of Chaos'**, London, England 1943

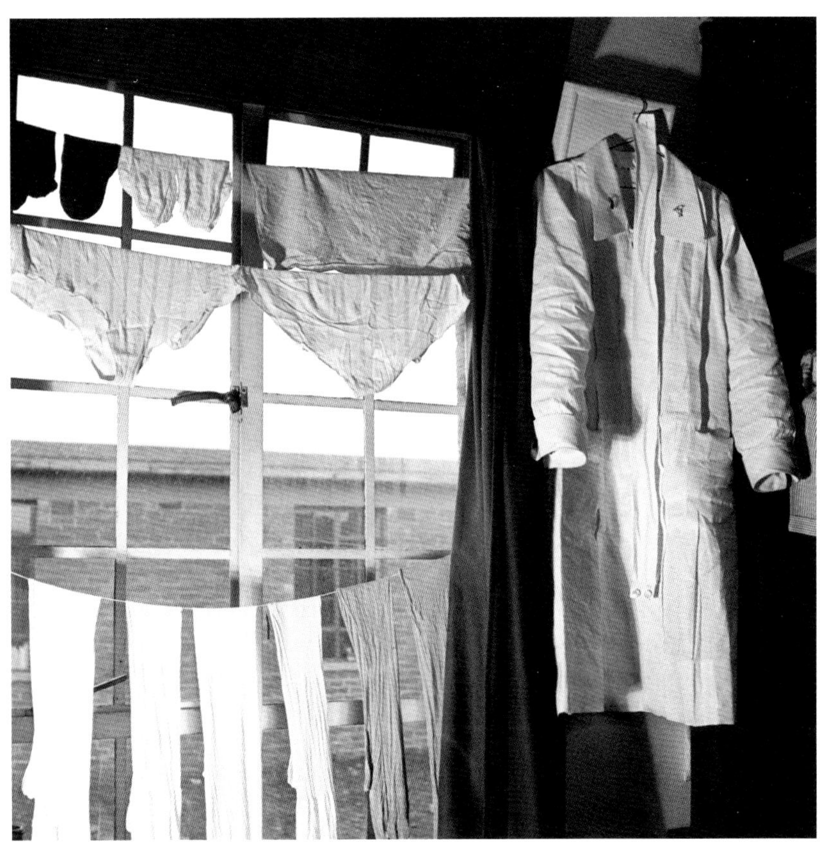

60 **US Army nurses' billet**, Churchill Hospital, Oxford, England 1943

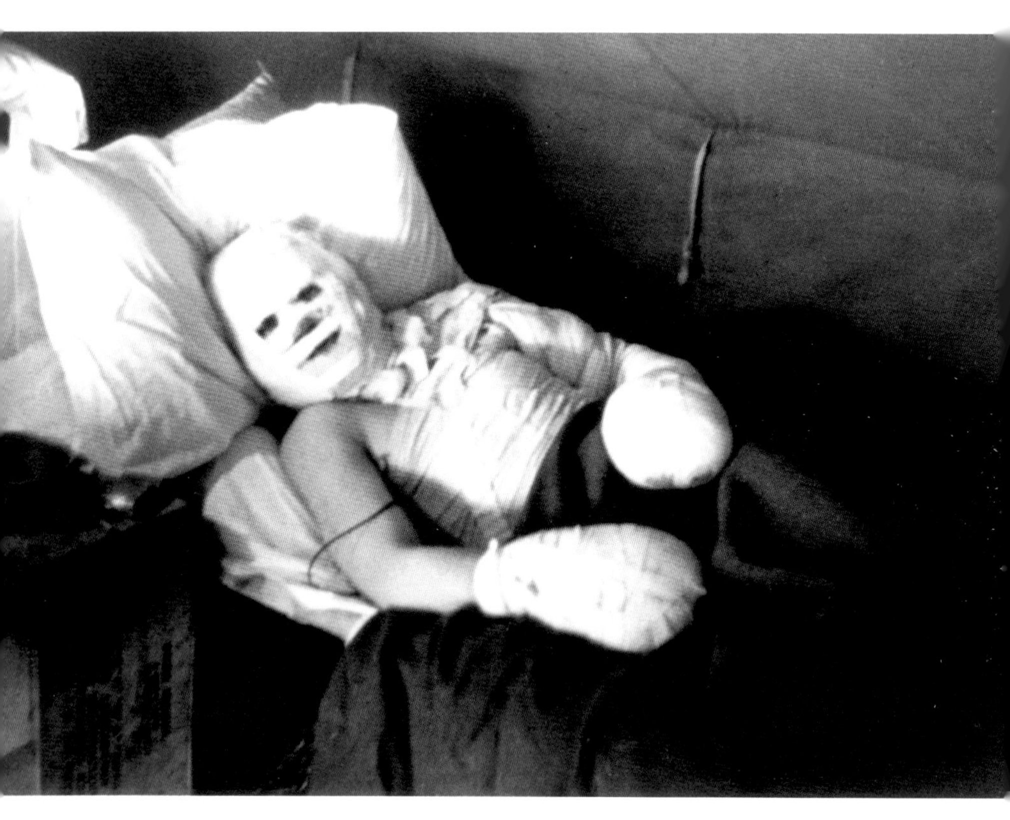

61 **Bad Burns Case**, Normandy, France 1944

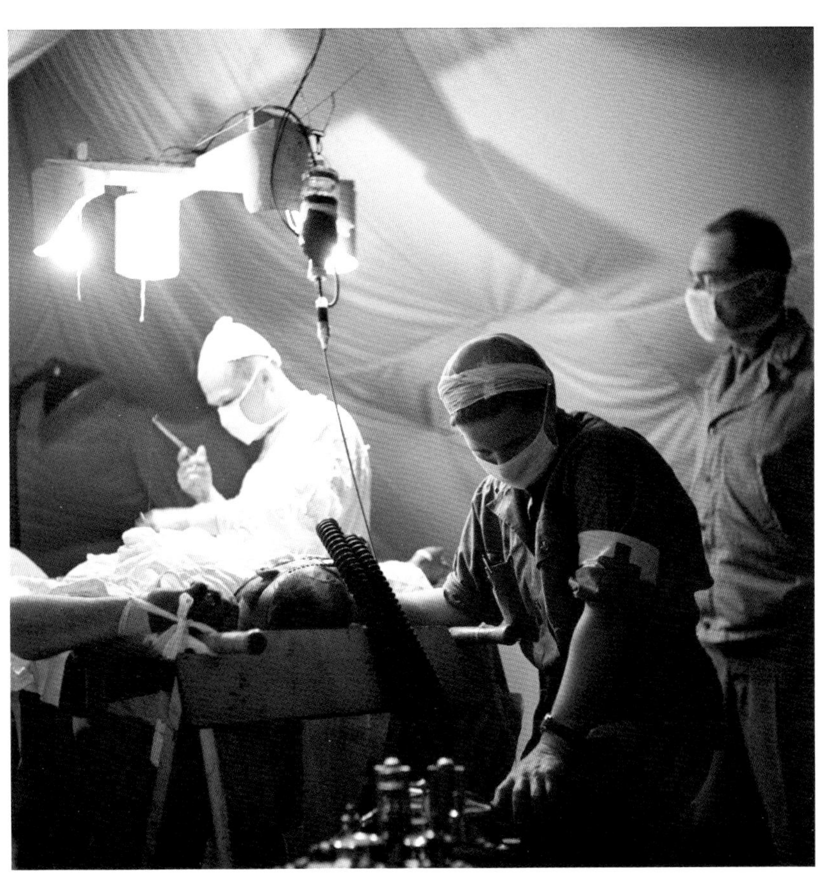

62 **Surgeon and anaesthetist at 44th Evacuation Hospital,**
Bricqueville, Normandy, France 1944

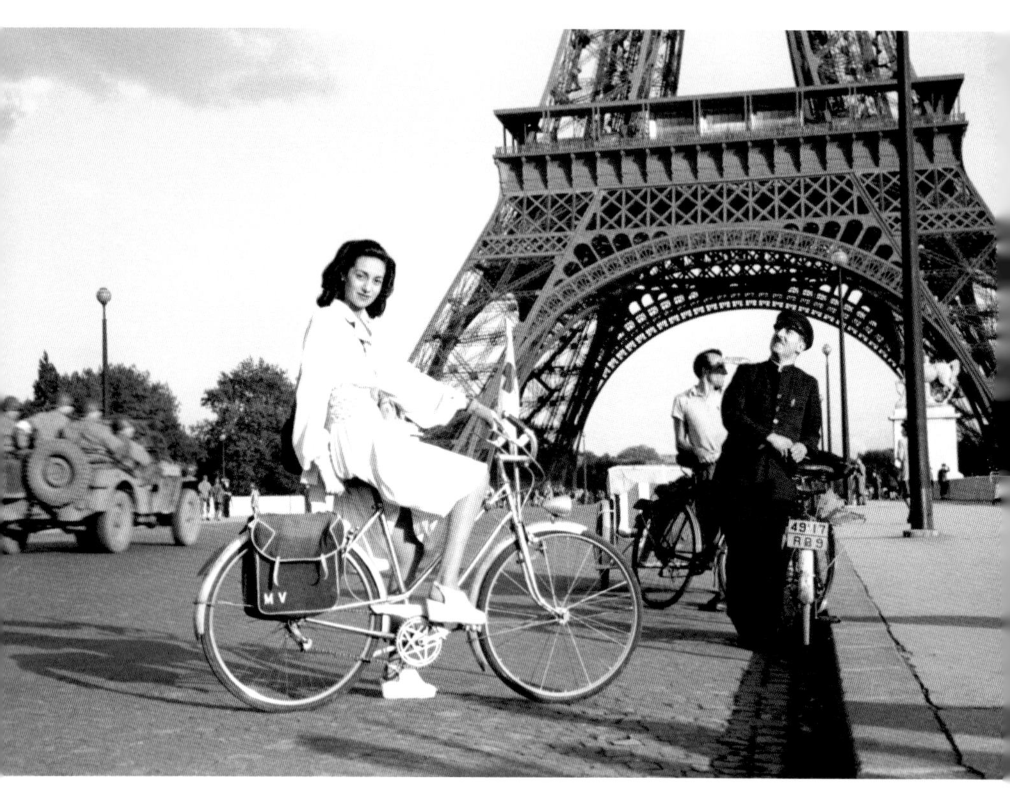

63 **For cycling:** Paris, France 1944

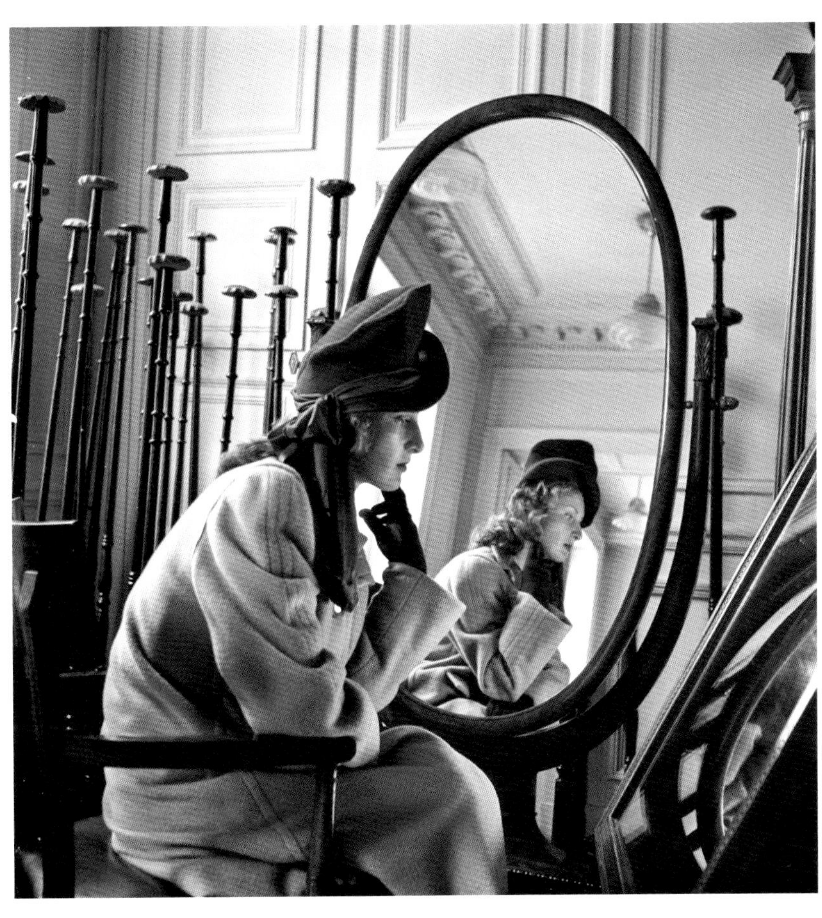

64 **Rose Descat's dark red felt hat**, Paris, France 1944

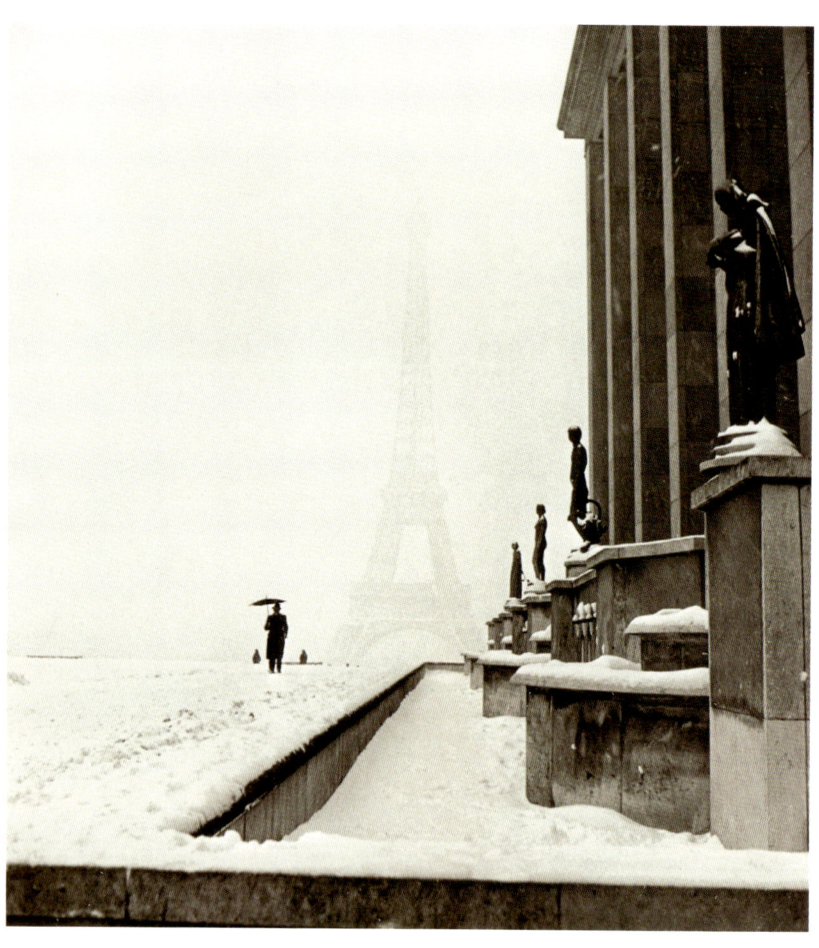

65 **The veiled Eiffel Tower from the Palais de Chaillot**, Paris, France 1944

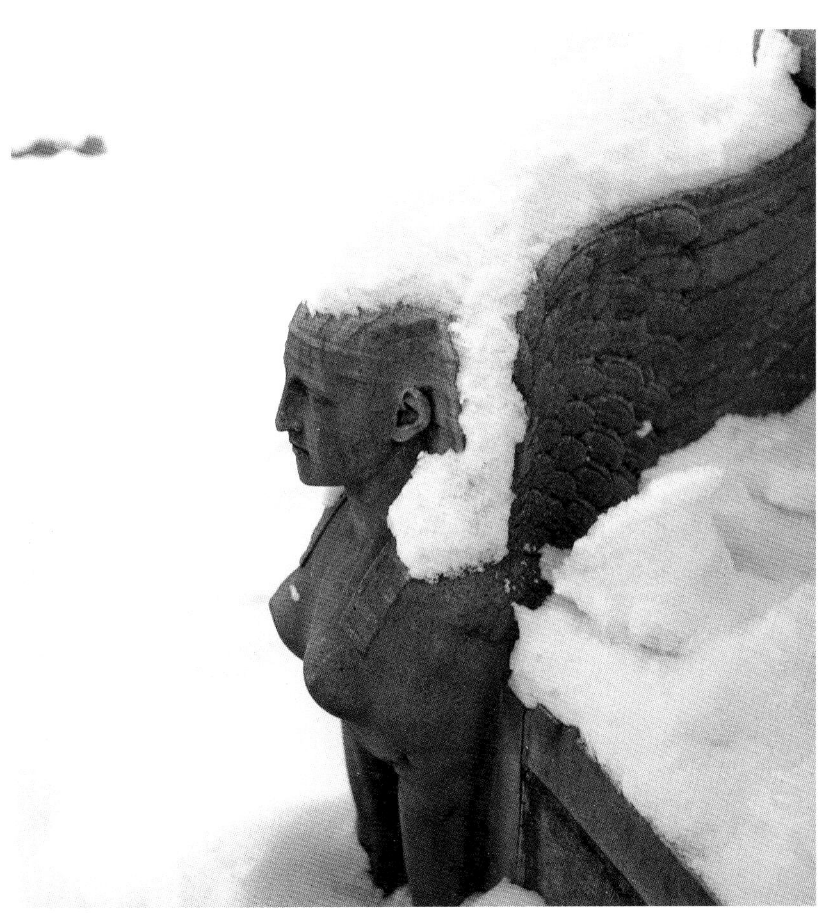

66 **Snow capped statue**, Jardins des Tuileries, Paris, France 1944

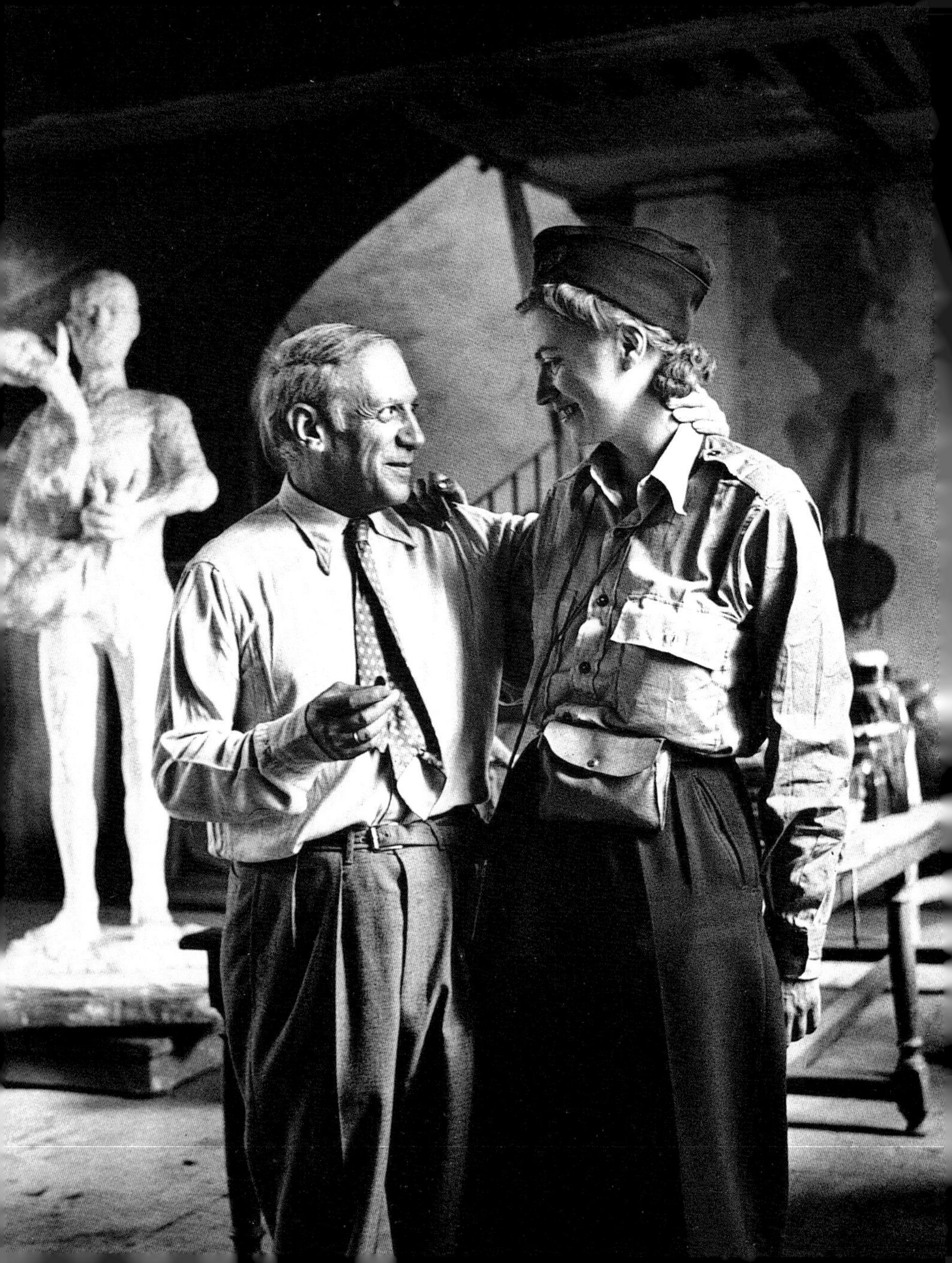

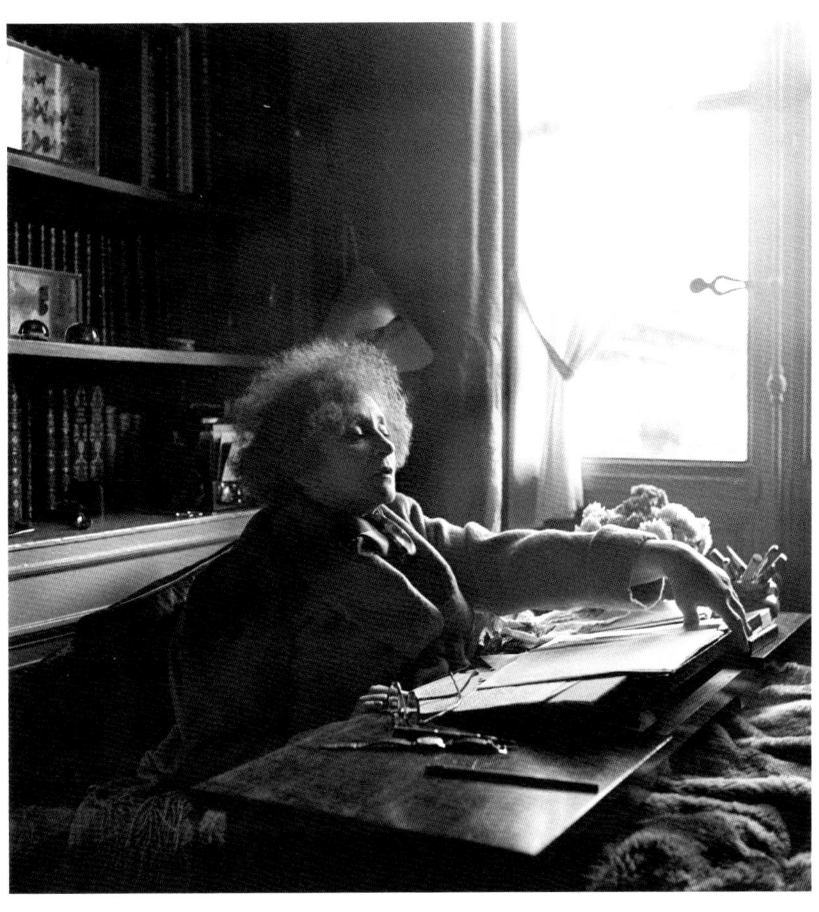

67 **Picasso and Lee Miller in his studio**, Paris, France 1944

68 **Colette**, Paris, France 1944

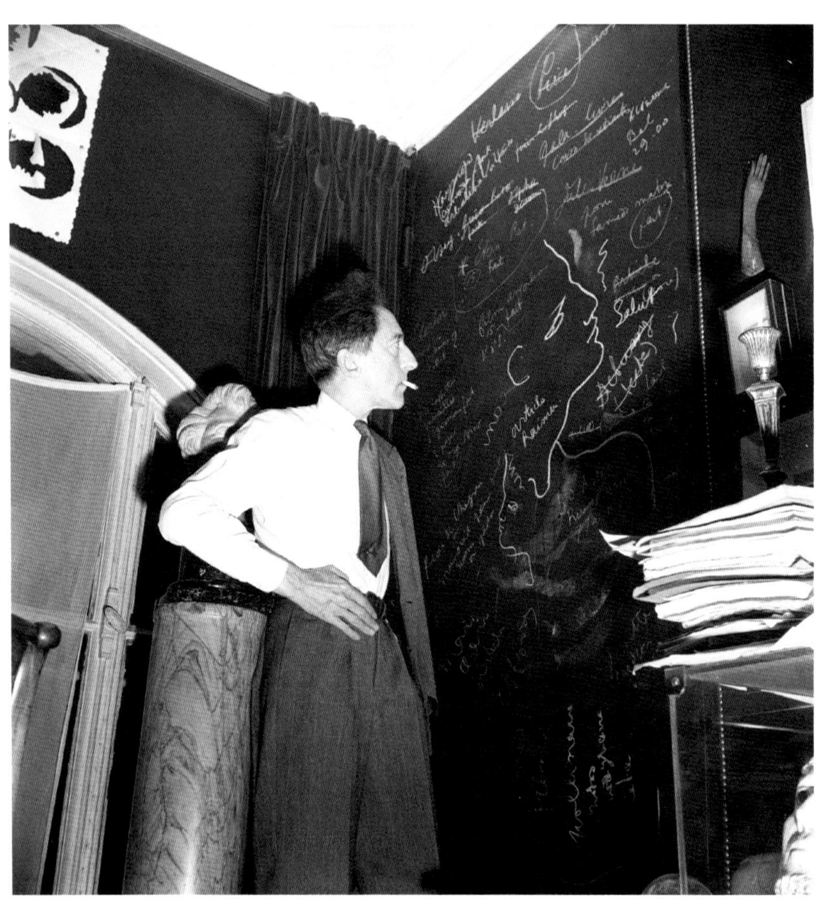

69 **Jean Cocteau at home**, Paris, France 1944

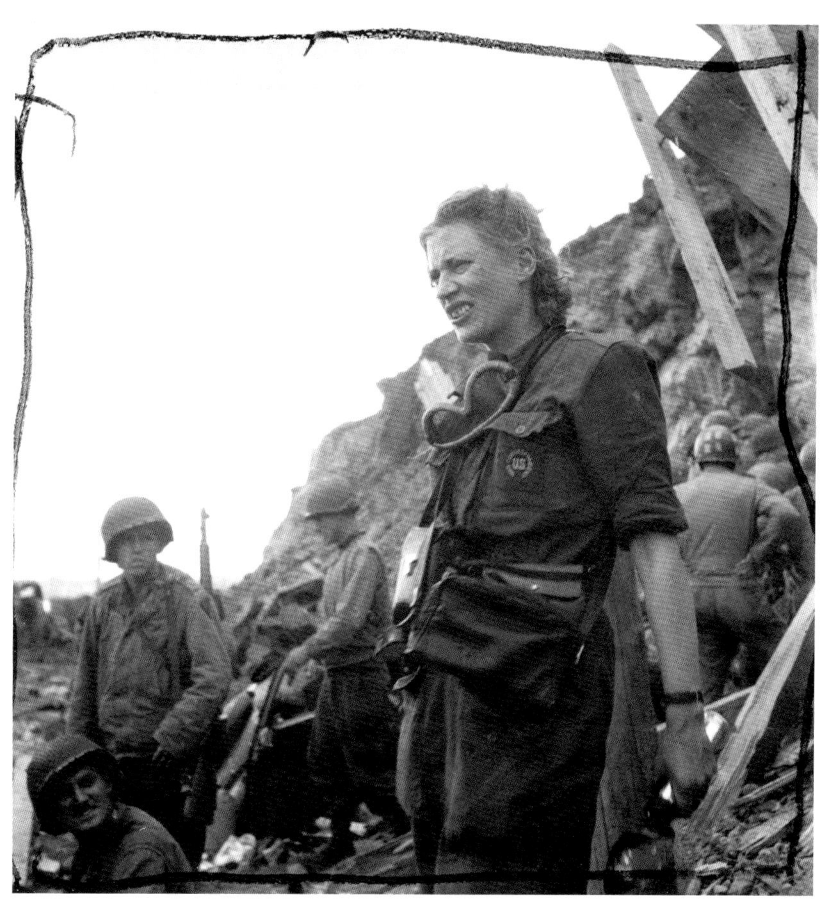

70 **Lee Miller at entrance to St Malo Fortress**, St Malo, France 1944

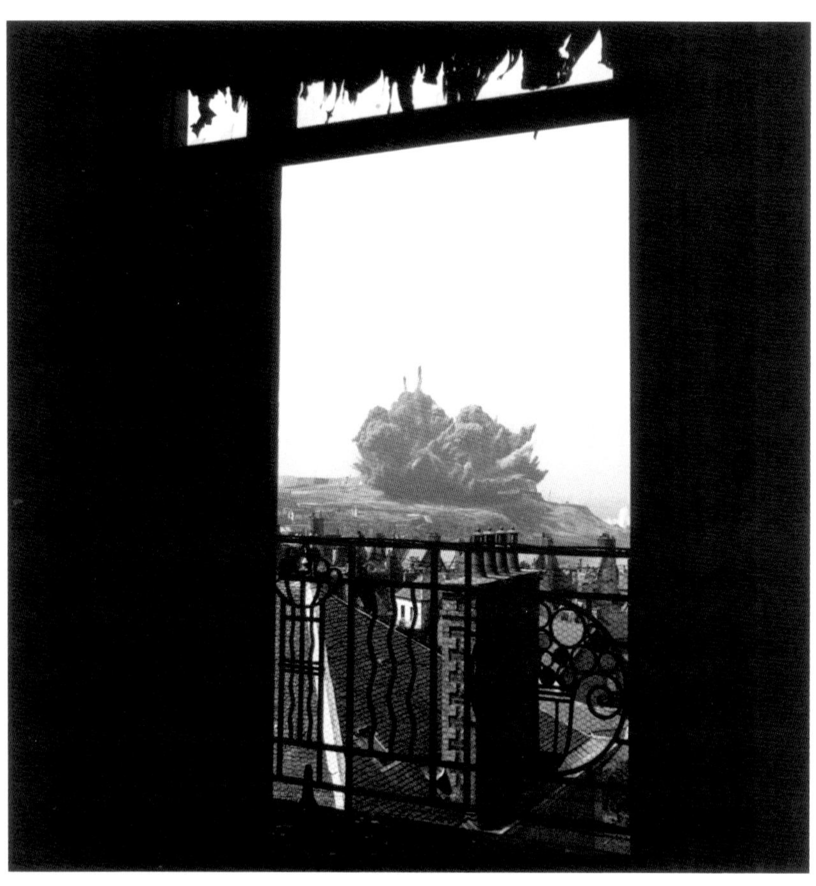

71 **Fall of the Citadel, Aerial bombardment**, St Malo, France 1944

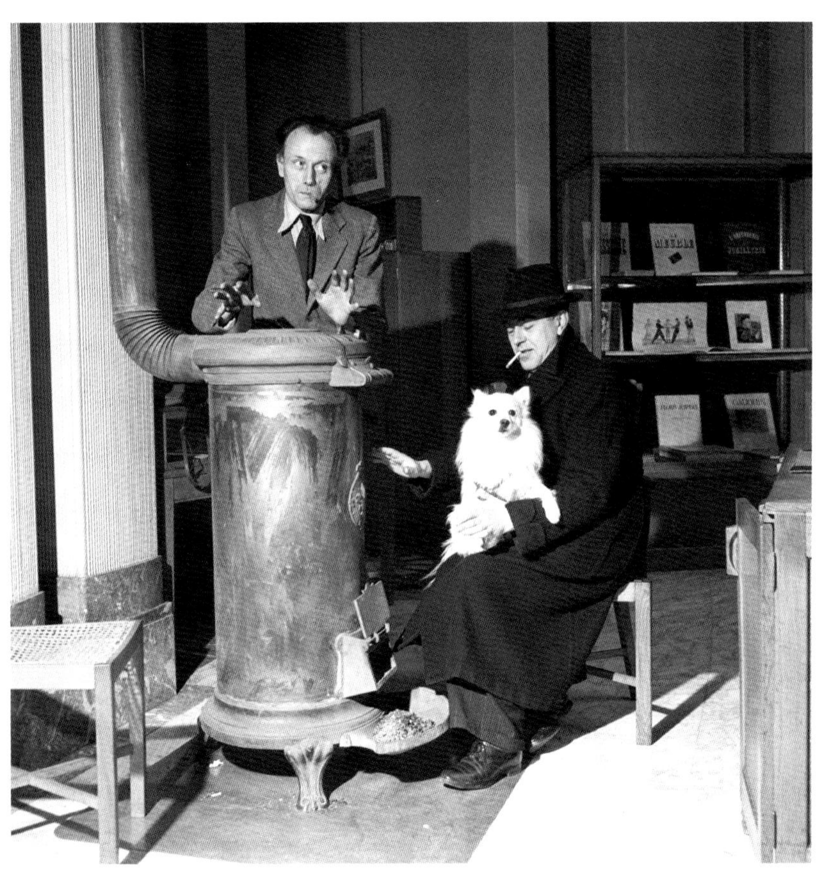

72 **Paul Delvaux and René Magritte**, Brussels, Belgium 1944

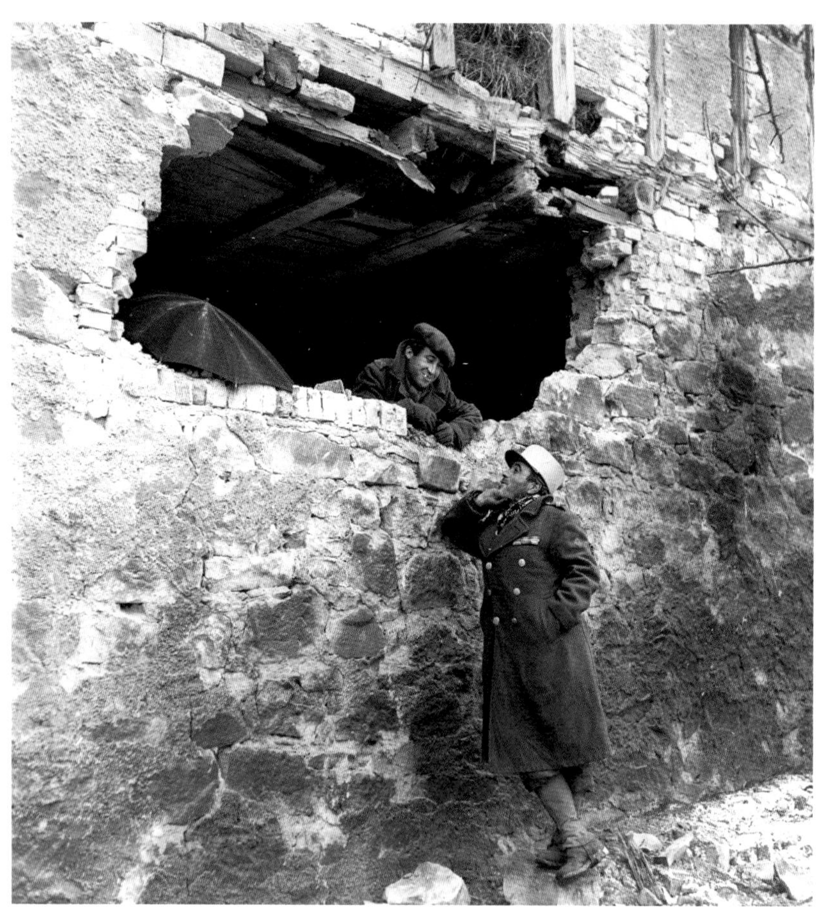

73 **Copains discussing the war**, Alsace, France 1945

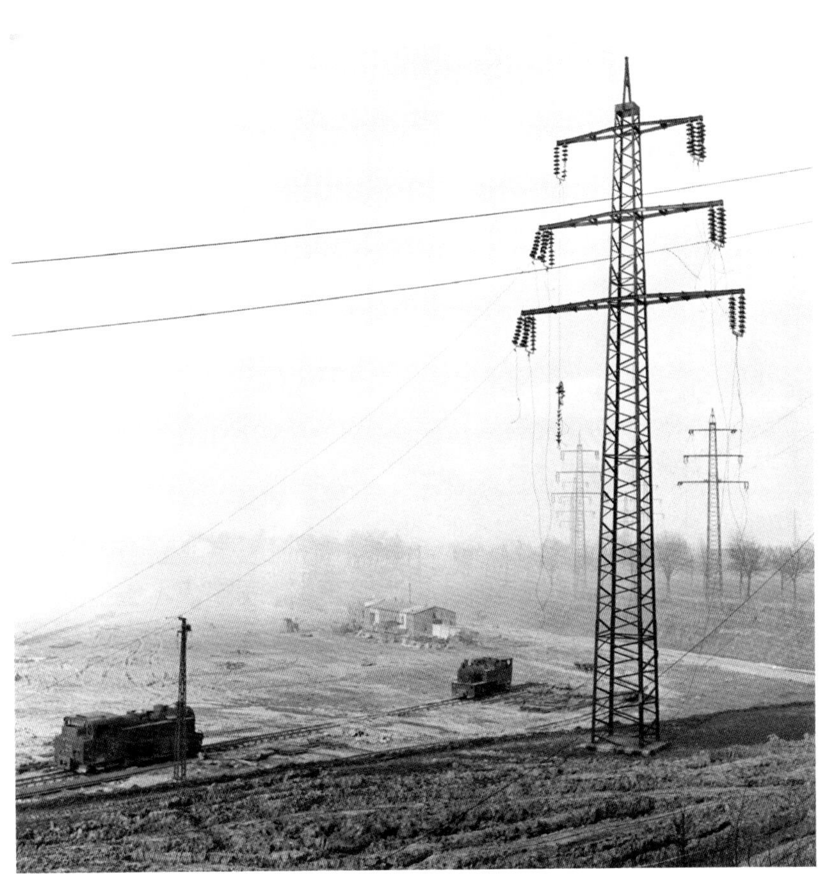

74 **Burning surface coal mines**, Duren, Germany 1945

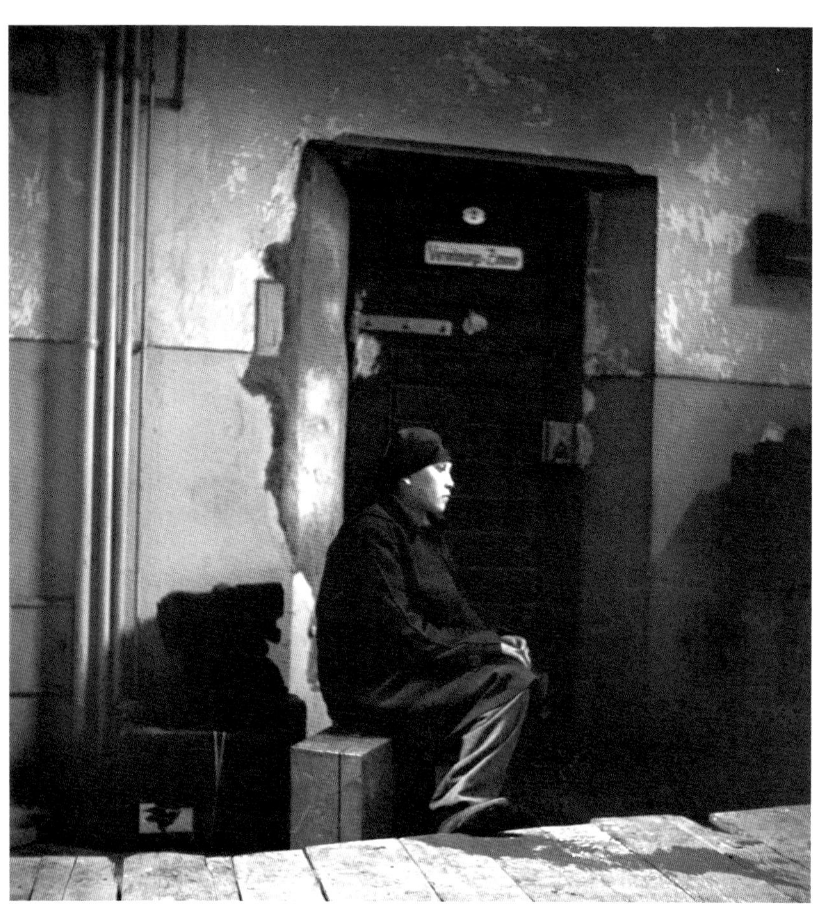

75 **Last Leap - The Rhine, Kingelputz prison**, Cologne, Germany 1945

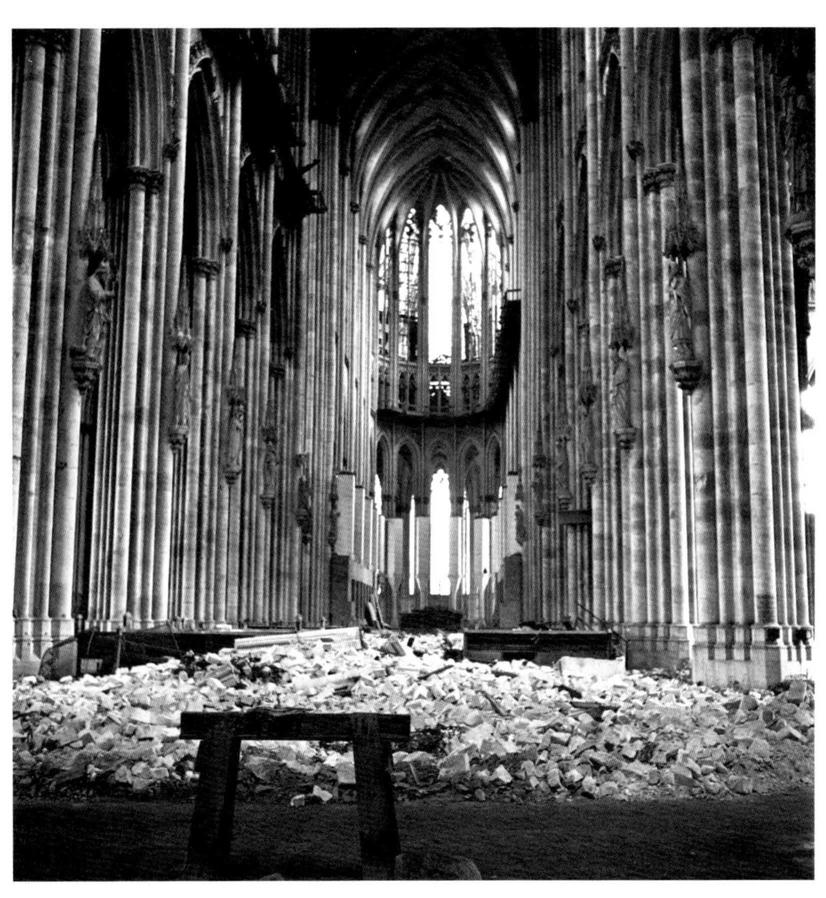

76 **Cologne Cathedral**, Cologne, Germany 1945

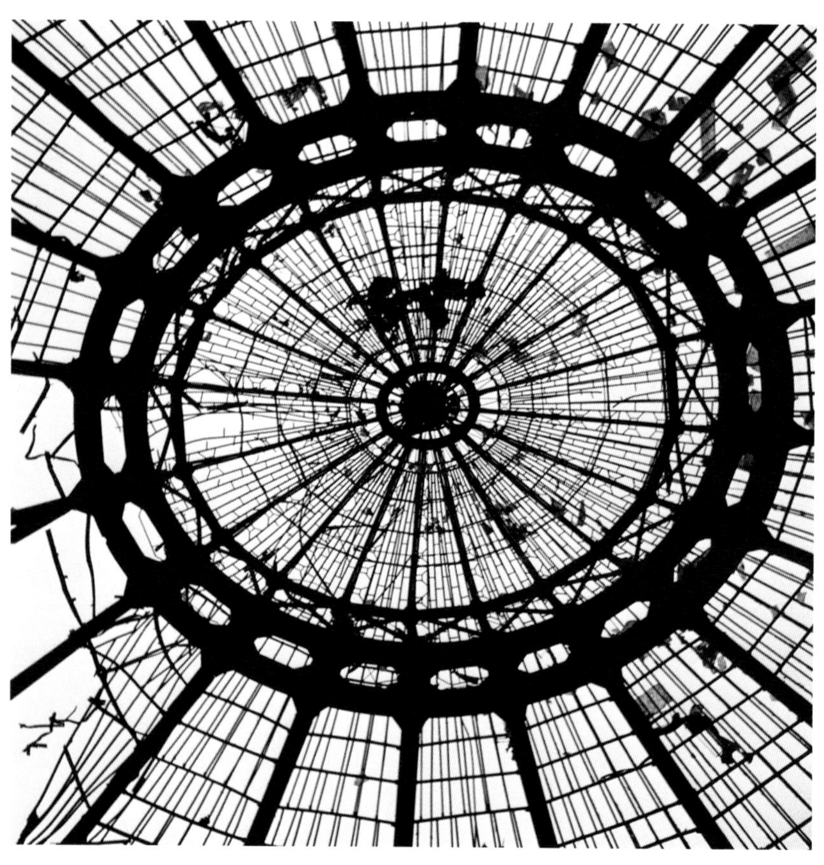

77 **Steel spiderweb - Roof of The Festhalle**, Frankfurt, Germany 1945

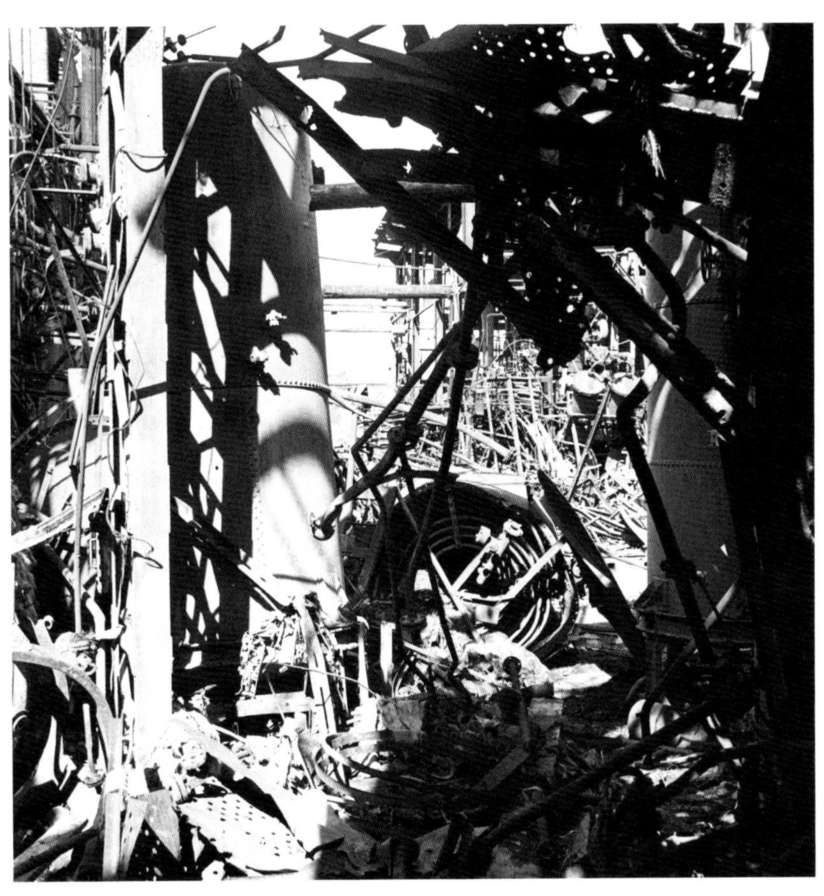

78 **Inside a great chemical plant**, Ludwigshaven, Germany 1945

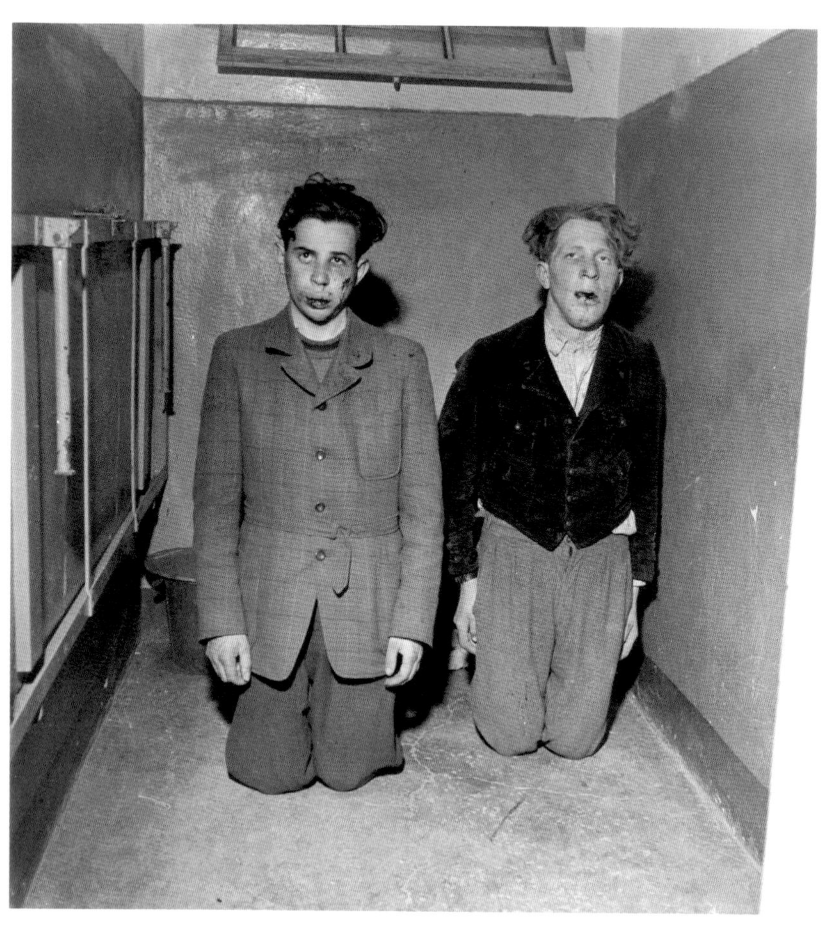

79 **Captured German guards**, Buchenwald, Germany 1945

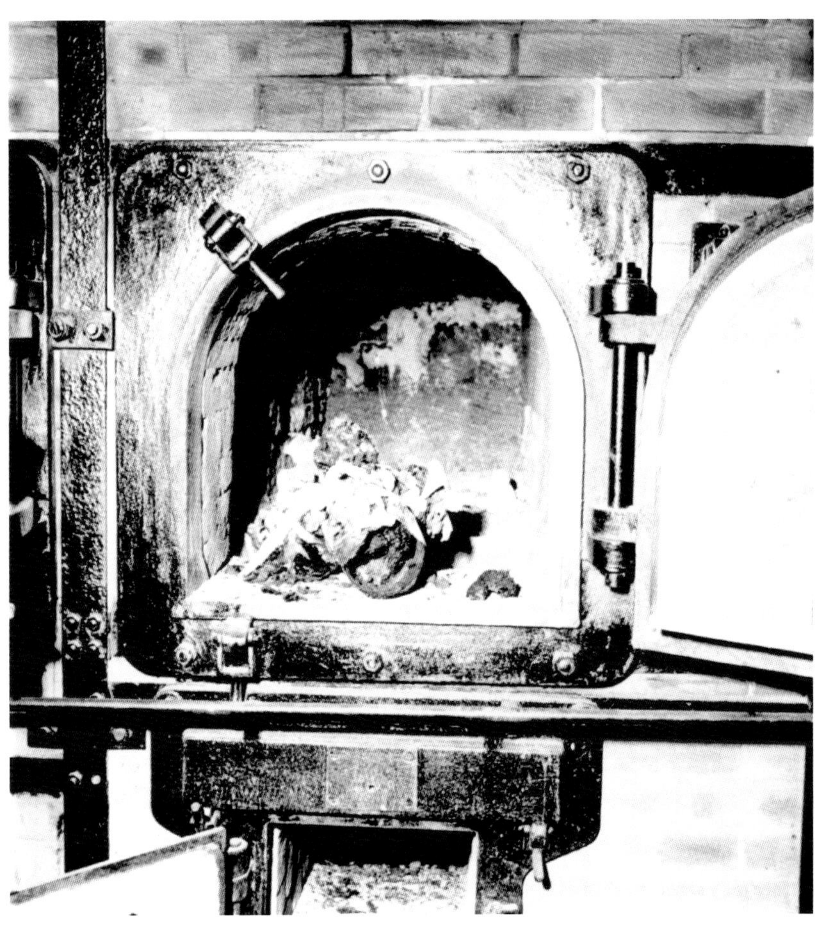

80 **Orderly furnaces of the crematorium**, Buchenwald, Germany 1945

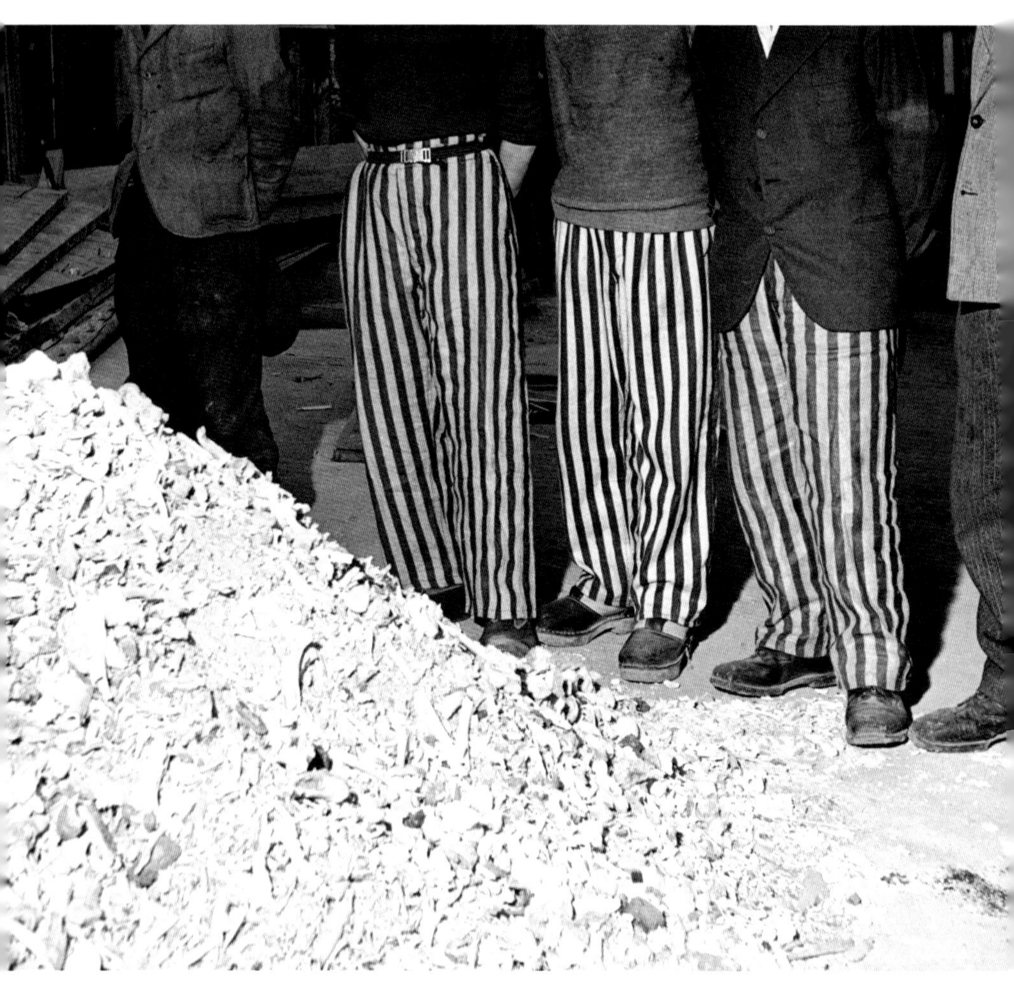

81 **Detail of released prisoners in striped prison dress...**, Buchenwald, Germany 1945

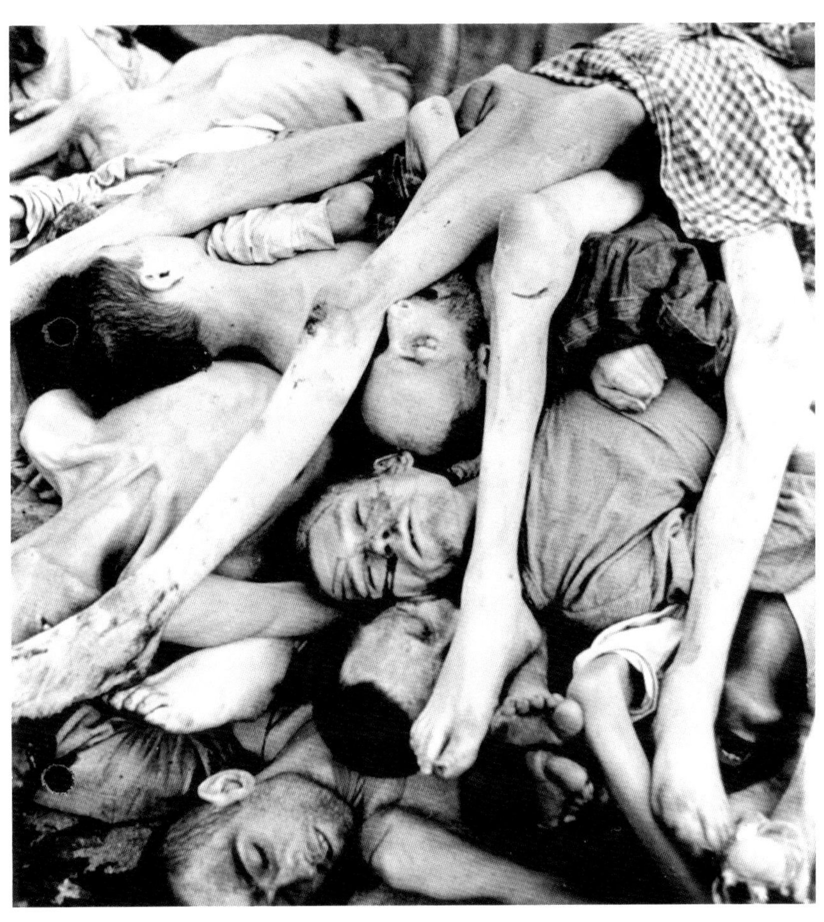

82 **Horrors of a concentration camp**, Buchenwald, Germany 1945

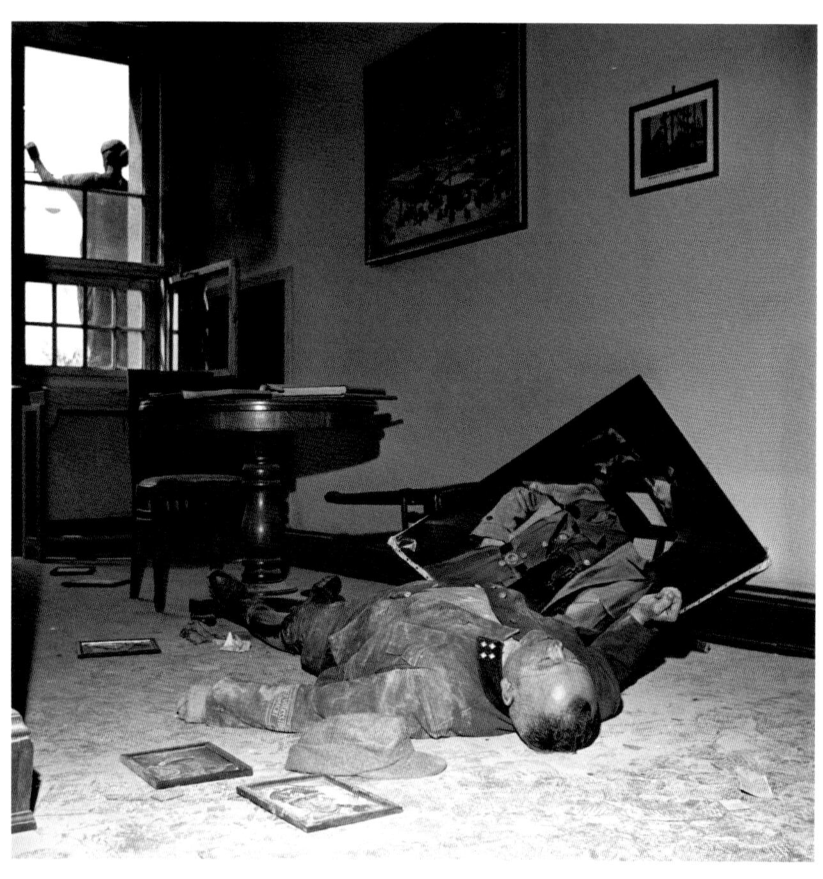

83 **Suicided Volkssturm Commander; Walter Doenicke,**
Town Hall, Leipzig, Germany 1945

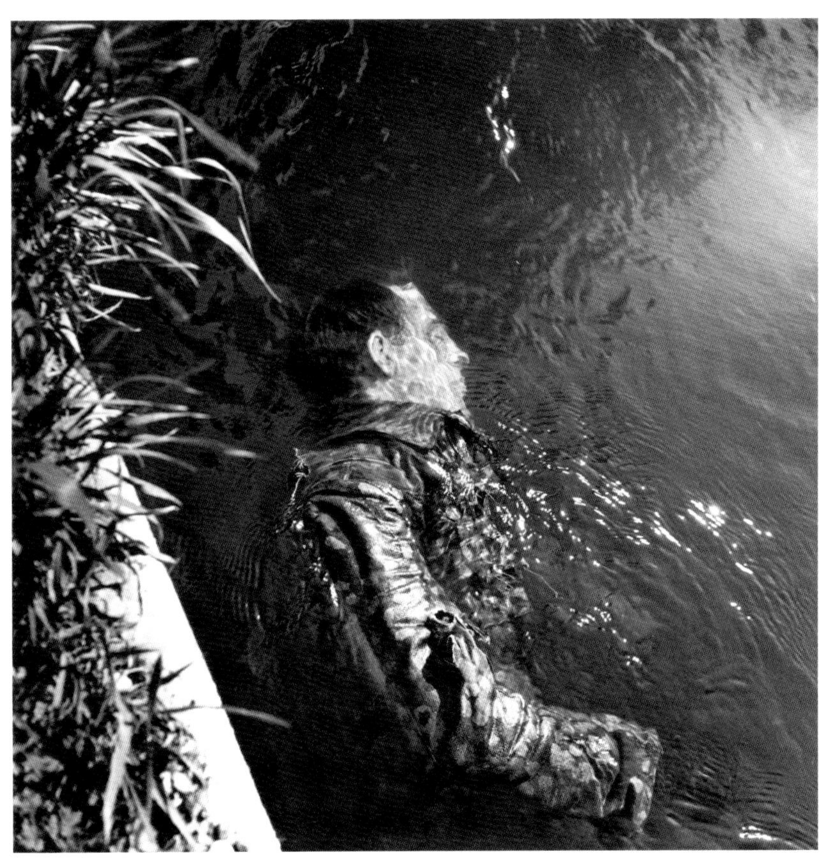

84 **Dead SS prison guard floating in canal**, Dachau, Germany 1945

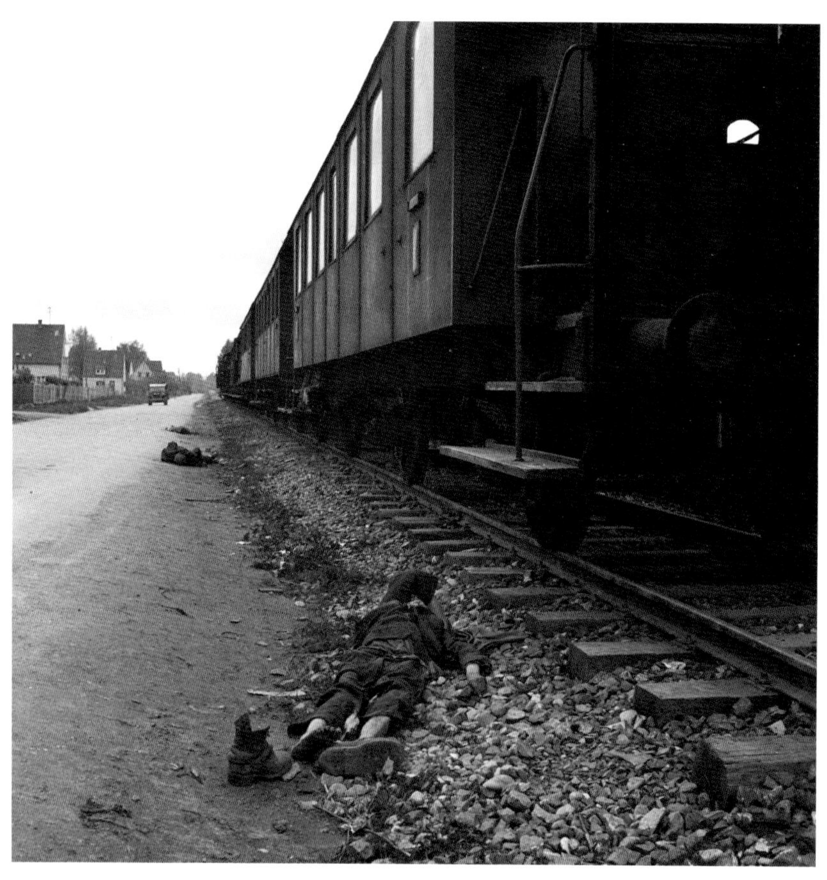

85 **Dead deportees lie beside the rail track**, Dachau, Germany 1945

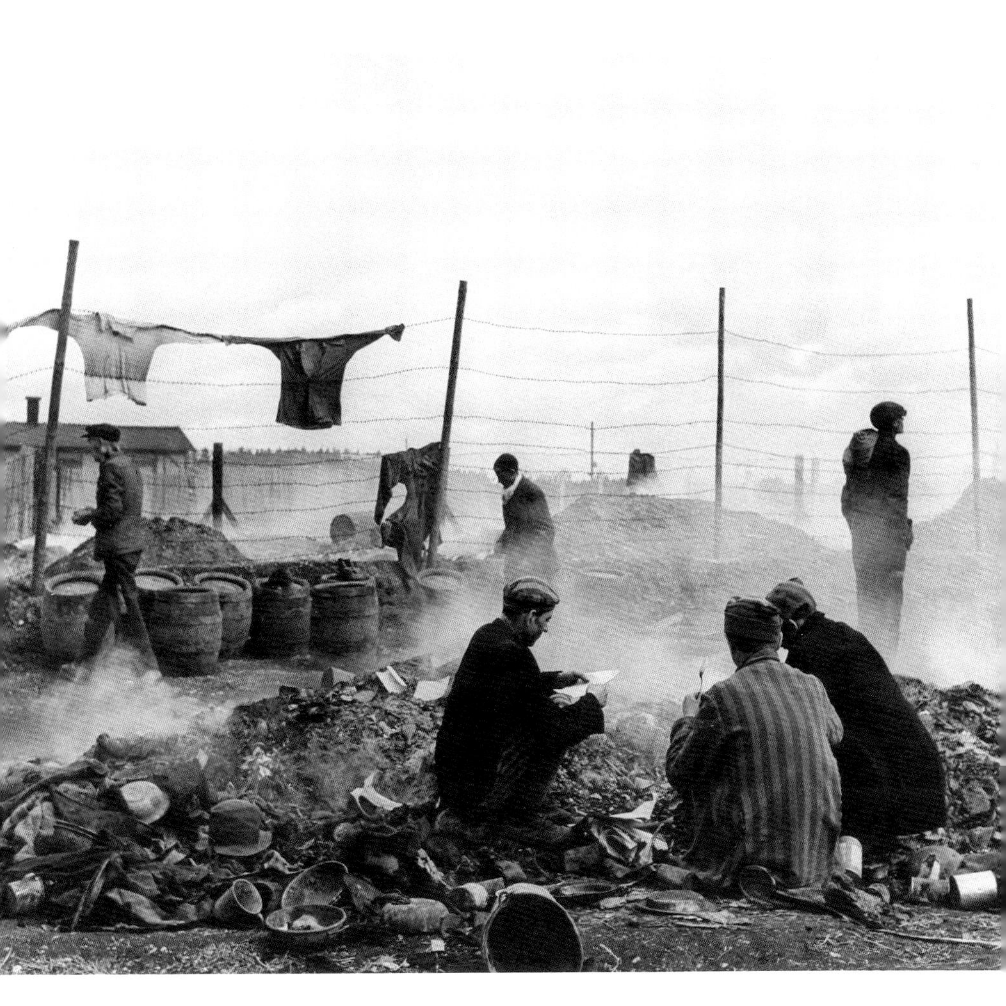

86 **Freed prisoners scavenging in the rubbish dump,**
Dachau Concentration Camp, Germany 1945

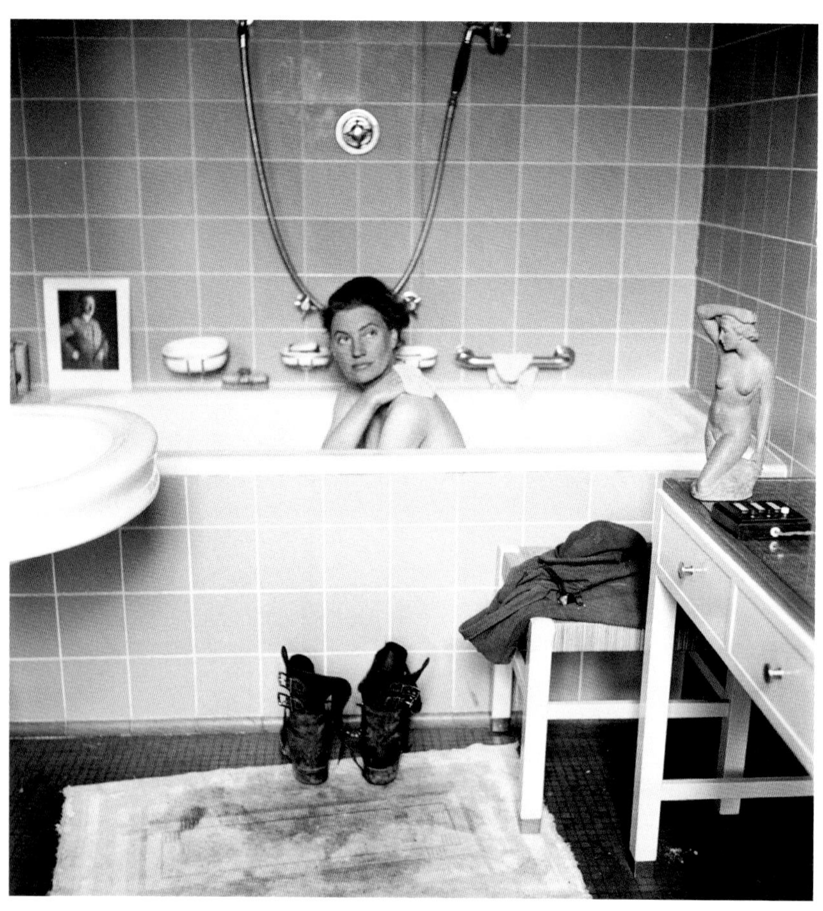

87 **Lee Miller in Hitler's bathtub**, Munich, Germany 1945

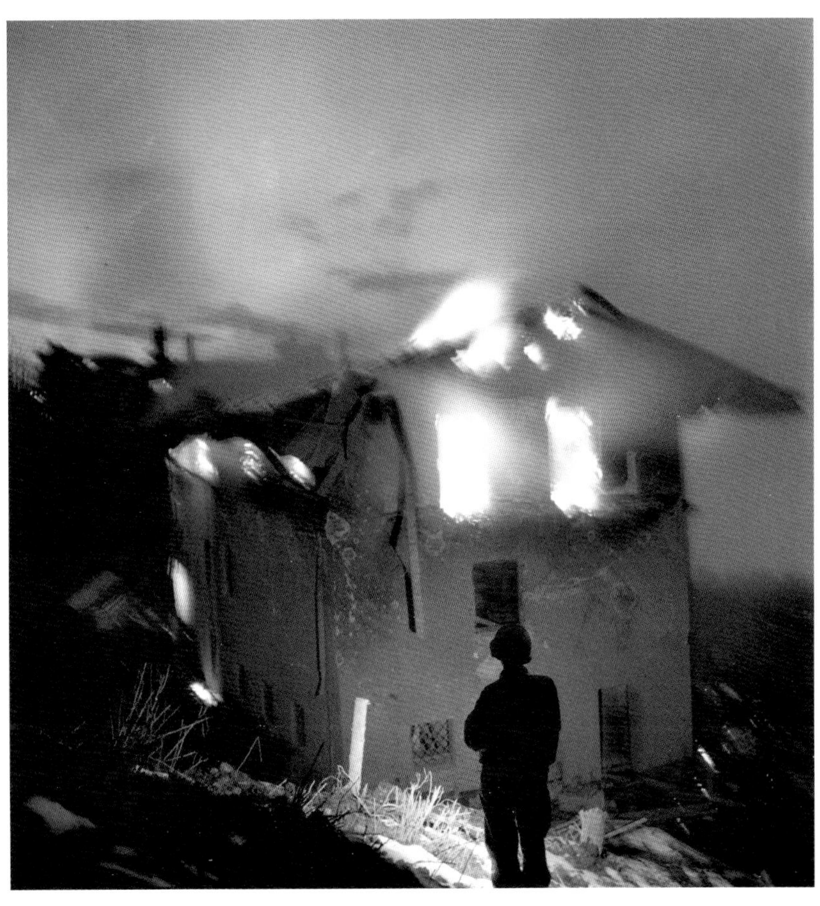

88 **Hitler's house [Berghof] on fire**, Obersalzberg, Bavaria, Germany 1945

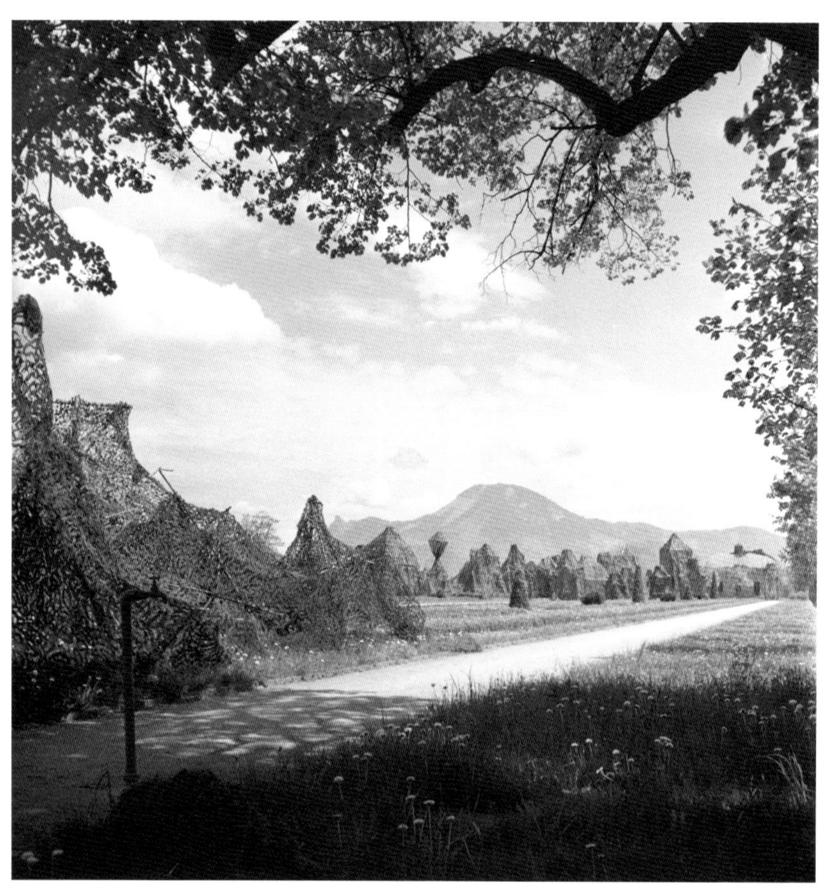

89 **Statues covered by camouflage nets, Schloss Klessheim**, Salzburg, Austria 1945

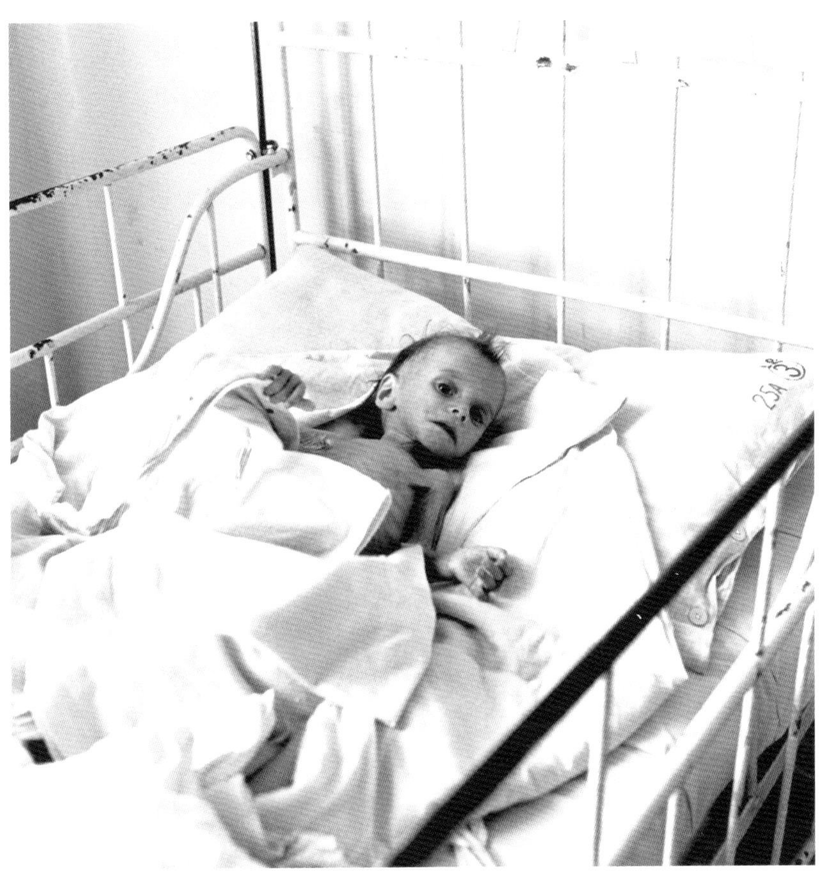

90 **Nearly all these children will die**, Wilhelminen hospital, Vienna, Austria 1945

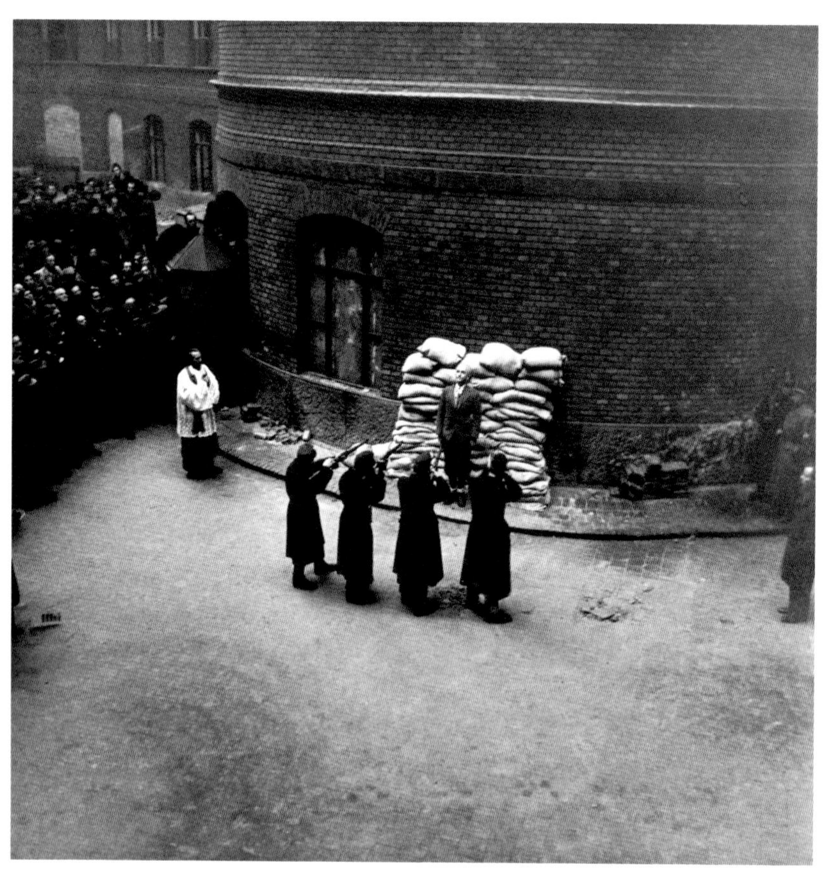

91 **Laszlo Bardossy, fascist ex-Prime Minister of Hungary, facing the firing squad**, Budapest, Hungary 1946

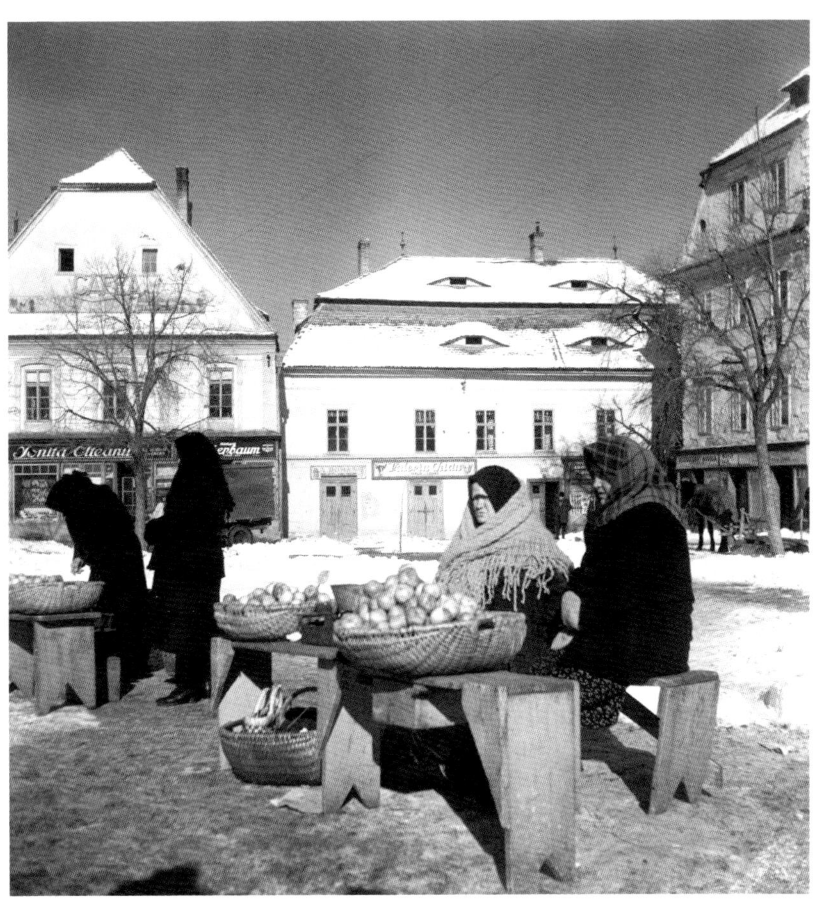

92 **'The eyes of Sibiu'**, Sibiu, Romania 1946

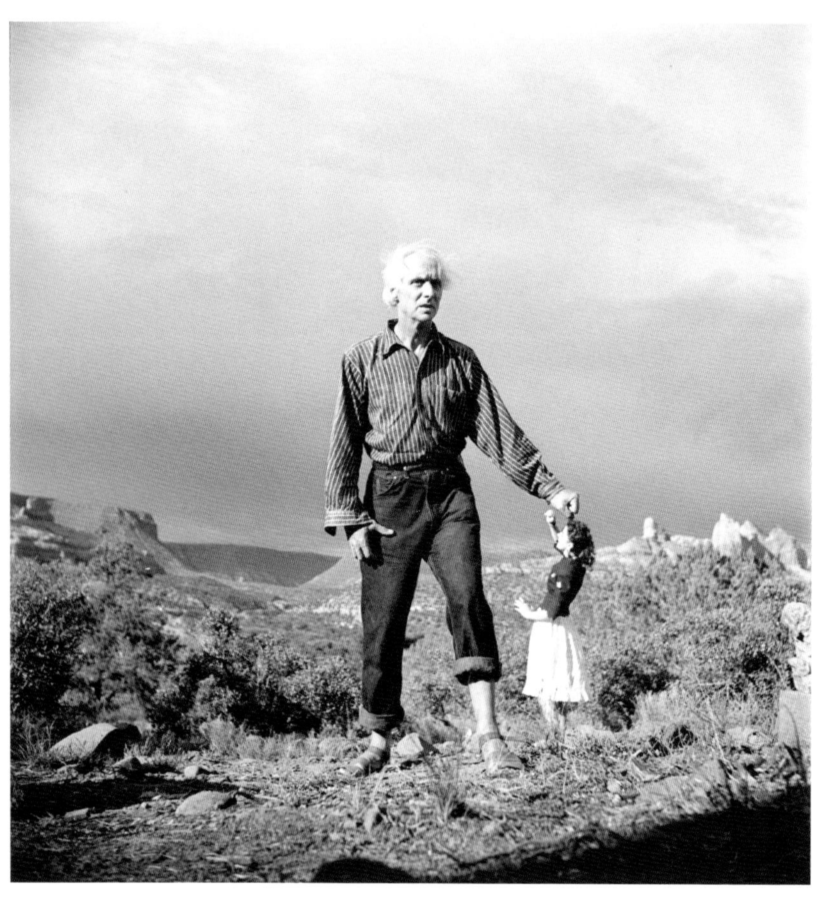

93 **Max Ernst and Dorothea Tanning**, Sedona, Arizona, USA 1946

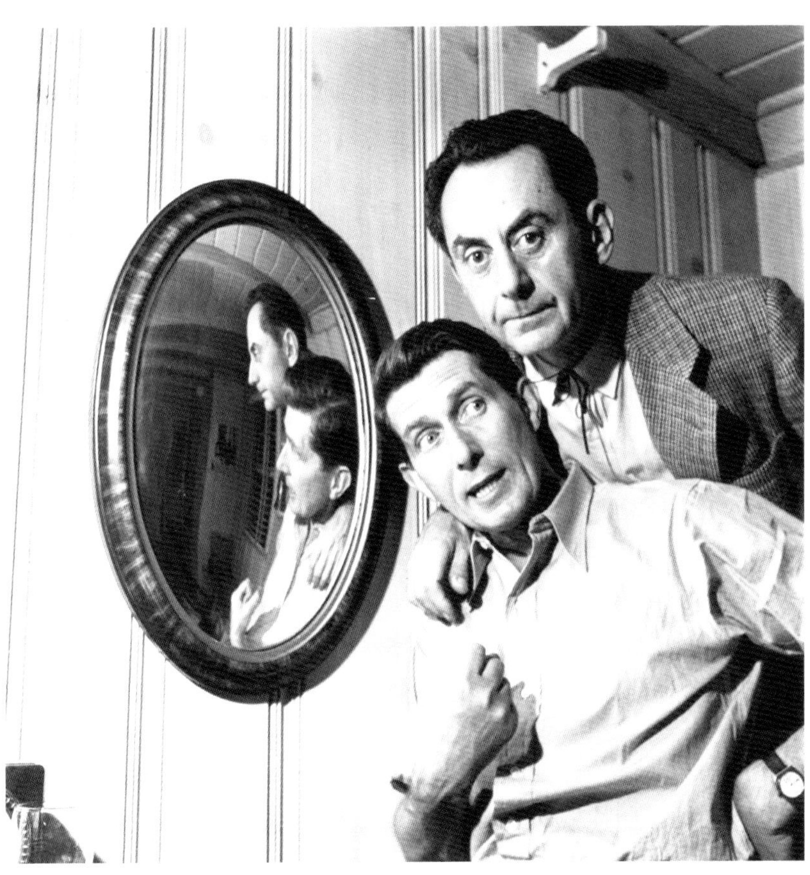

94 **Roland Penrose with Man Ray**, Los Angeles, USA 1946

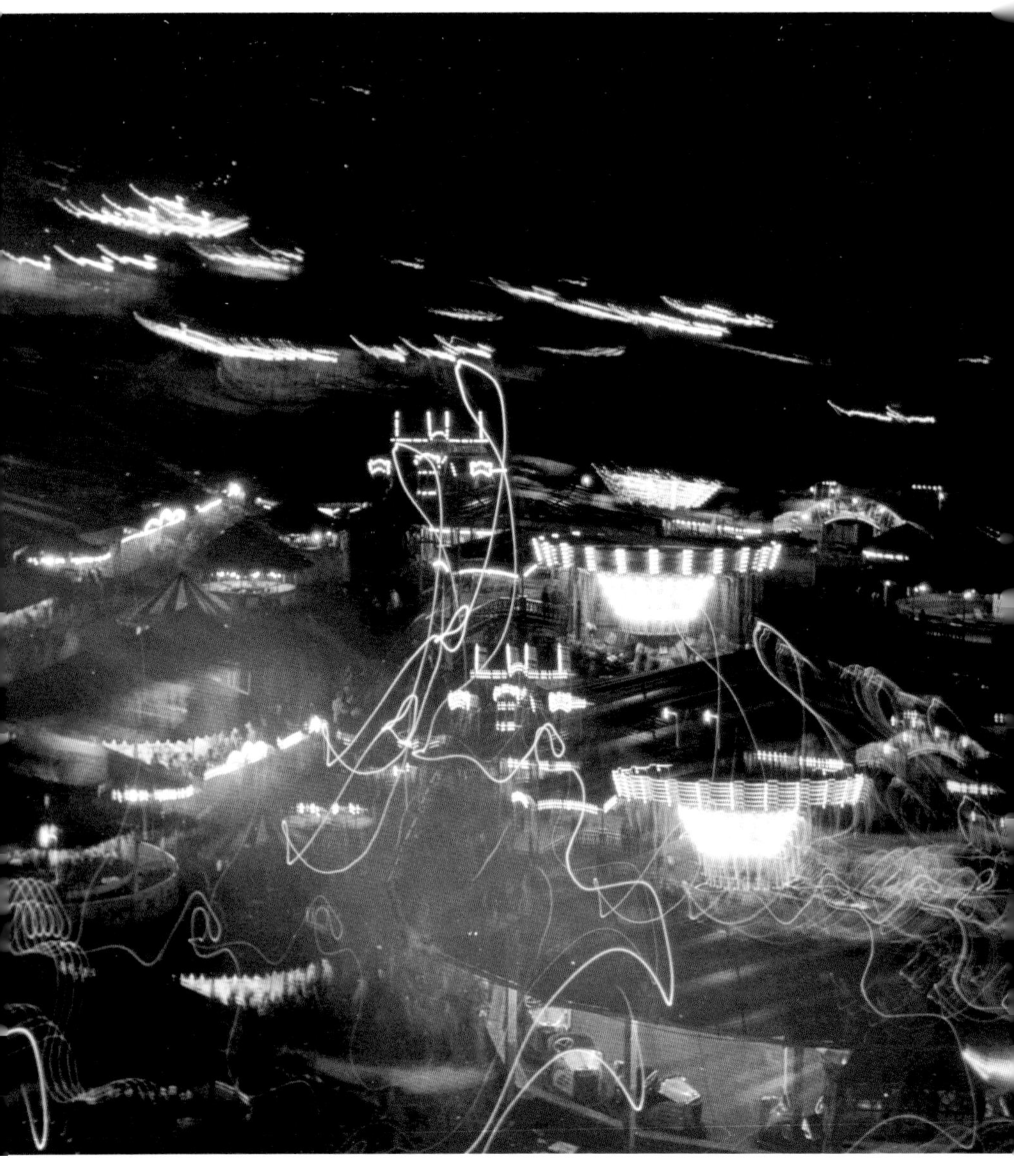

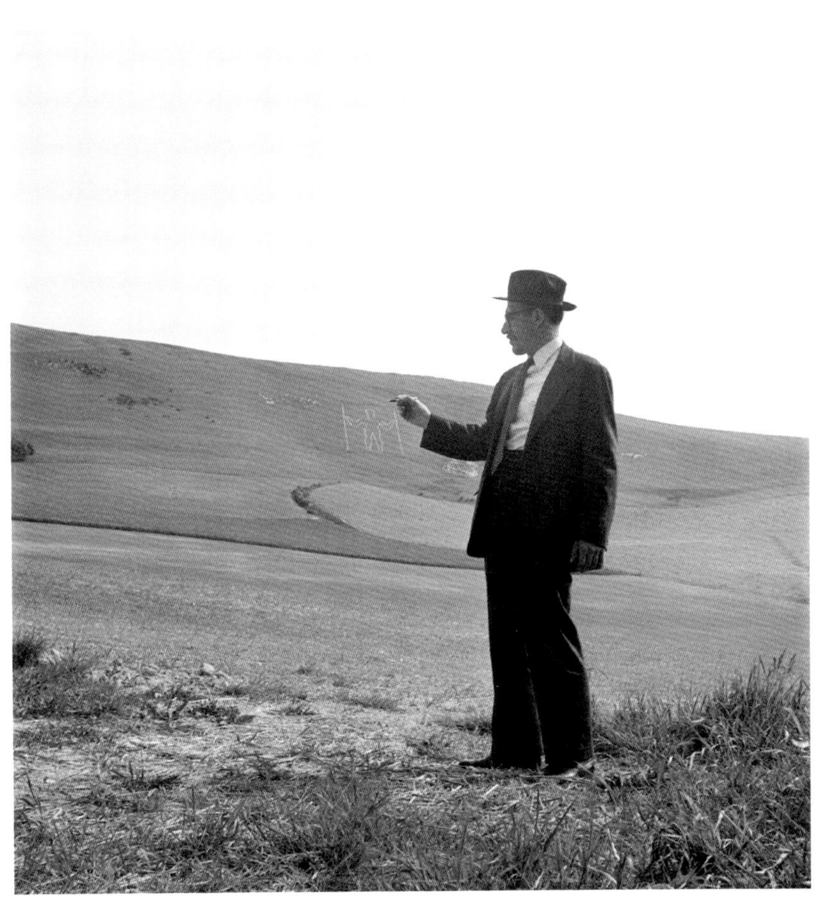

95 **Hampstead Fair**, London, England 1949

96 **Saul Steinberg, Long Man of Wilmington**, East Sussex, England 1952

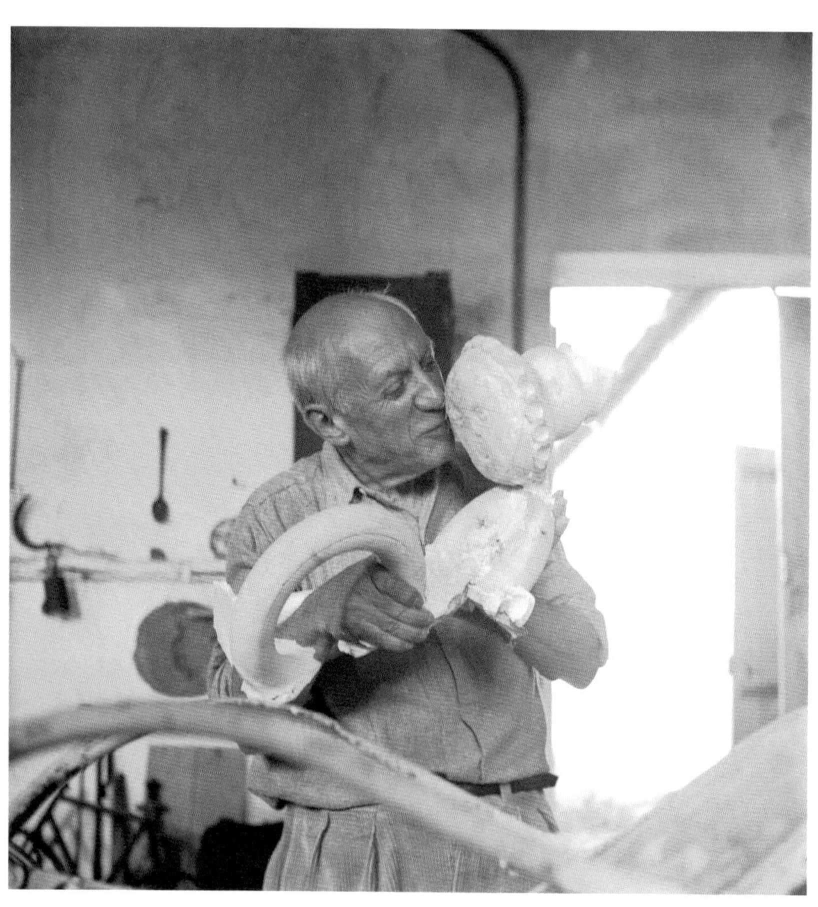

97 **Picasso embracing his sculpture**, Vallauris, France 1954

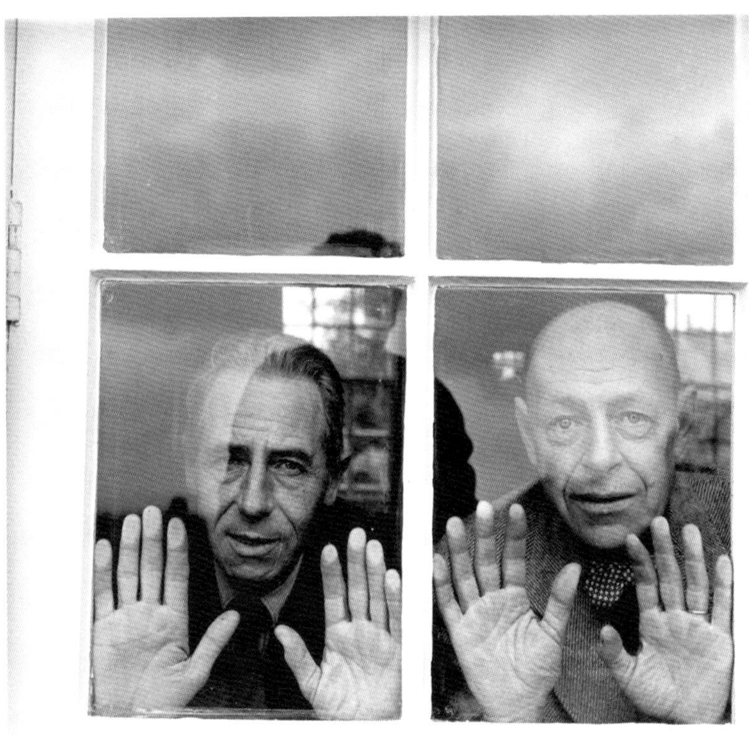

98 **Georges Limbour and Jean Dubuffet**, Farleys House, England 1955

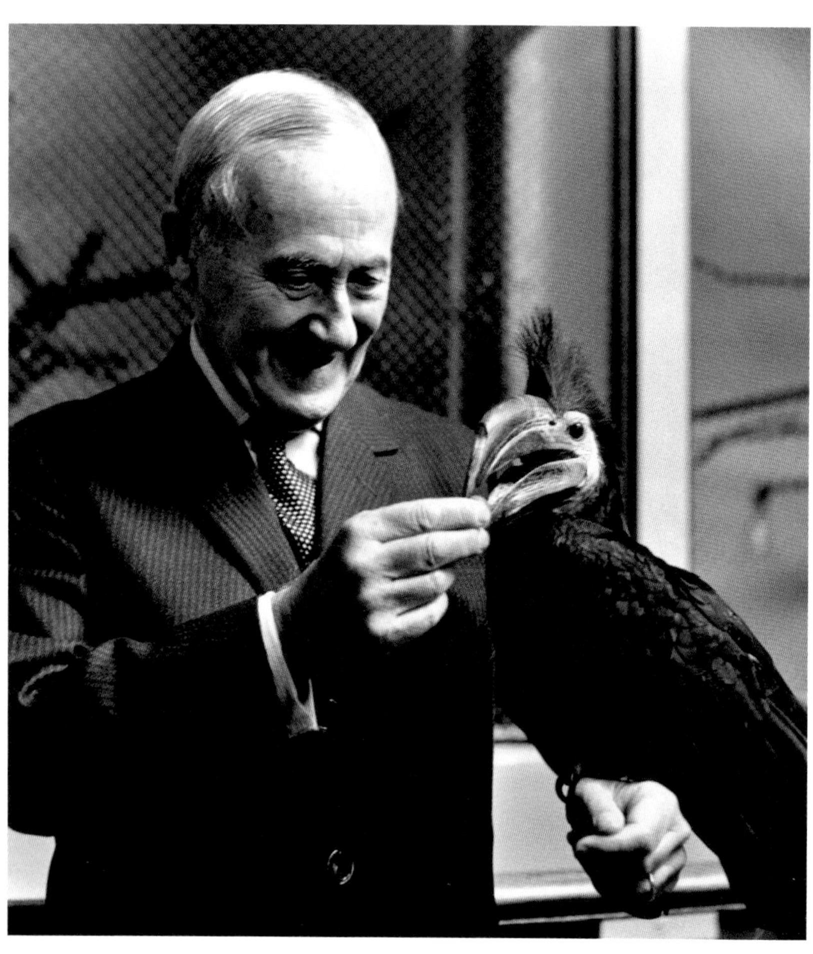

99 **Miró at the zoo [Hornbill]**, London, England 1964

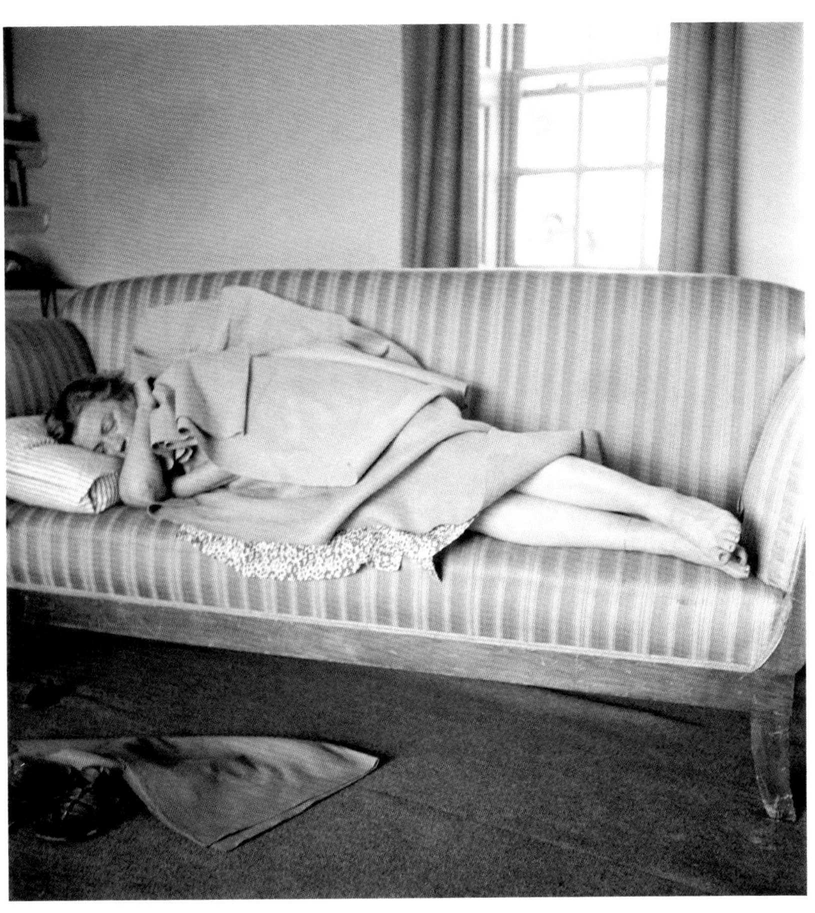

100 **Lee Miller the hostess takes it easy**, Farleys House, England 1953

SURREALIST LEE MILLER

NOTES ON IMAGES

01 **Man Ray shaving,** Paris, France 1929 (NC0140-3)

The American Man Ray was the pre-eminent Surrealist photographer in Paris. Lee Miller became his pupil, lover and muse from 1928 to 1932. He introduced her to Surrealism and taught her photography and she inspired and modelled for some of his best known works.

02 **Untitled [Severed breast from radical surgery in a place setting 1]**, Paris, France c1929

Lee Miller acquired the breast whilst working as a technical photographer for a surgeon in Paris. She then set up this shot in *Vogue Studios* but was discovered by George Hoyningen-Heuné who threw her and the breast out in the street.

03 **Untitled [Sabots on parched earth]**, Paris, France c1930 (NC0057-8)

Lee Miller never had a strong affinity with rural life, but this picture speaks with an eloquent understanding of drought. It shows us how she developed strong powers of observation early on in her work, choosing to use details to make her statements.

04 **Untitled [Man and tar]**, Paris, France c1930

For some the spilled tar becomes the man's cape, dropped on the road. For others the man is about to step into the jaws of a giant black manta ray. The ambiguity is intentional and open to many other interpretations.

05 **Untitled [Rat tails]**, Paris, France c1930 (NC0057-7)

The rats have turned their backs on us. Perhaps they have important things to discuss, but the vulnerability of their dangling tails suggest we may be invading their privacy just by looking at them.

06 **Untitled [Carousel cows]**, Paris, France c1930 (NC0057-6)

Cows with extravagant horns loom up over us. Although part of a children's carousel the animals have a threatening look, perhaps even nightmarish. Dreams were seen by the surrealists as valuable insights into the realm of the subconscious.

07 **Untitled [Nude wearing a sabre guard]**, Paris, France c1930 (NC0105-12)

The wire mesh sabre guard is a device intended to protect swordsmen during training and competition. Here it contrasts with the soft vulnerability of the woman's body and exposed throat, leading us to wonder if it would provide adequate protection from an attack with a sabre.

08 **Nude bent forward, [thought to be Noma Rathner]**, Paris, France c1930 (NC0109-2)

Lee Miller constantly resisted the commodification of women and her female nudes capture the beauty and strength of the woman's body yet offer a less sexualised portrayal than might be expected from a male photographer.

09 **Untitled [Woman and child in clinic]**, Paris, France c1930 (NC0063-8)

The background figures are a mural in a clinic, but the woman and her baby are real. Dressed in white, the baby blends seamlessly with the mural, thus blurring the distinction between reality and illusion in a way the Surrealists loved.

10 **Tanja Ramm under a bell jar**, Paris, France 1930 (NC0103-8)

Lee Miller's inspiration for this photograph was probably her objection to the way some men regard women as a status enhancing trophies. Man Ray collaborated with Lee in making the photograph, and published his own version in Surréalisme au Service de la Révolution 2, 1930, titled Hommage á D. A. F. de Sade. The image reappears in a painting of his titled Aline et Velcour, 1950.

11 **Condom**, Paris, France c1930

We may be so intrigued by the visual puzzle of this image we forget that photographing a condom as a work of art was in itself a statement of defiance of the prevailing culture of France, and an assertion of the liberation of women.

12 **Guerlain shopfront**, 68 Avenue des Champs-Elysées, Paris, France c1930 (G0005)

Today the fashion house of Guerlain does not appear to be selling sensual perfumes or haute couture. Instead the elegant windows are full of foliage.

13 **Untitled [Exploding hand]**, Guerlain Parfumarie, Paris, France 1931 (G0002)

The woman's hand appears to have detonated in a puff of smoke. Closer examination reveals the 'explosion' is an opaque area on the glass made by the combined scratches of the diamond rings on the hands of Guerlain's customers.

14 **Untitled [Caged Birds]**, Paris, France 1931 (NC0046-2)

Two small birds are separately imprisoned in individual cages, further parted by flowers. The outside world is held at bay by heavy, elaborate ironwork. Lee Miller invites you to use the metaphors in whatever way you choose.

15 **Untitled [Impasse des deux anges]**, Paris, France c1931 (NC0063-9)

The image is difficult to reconcile with the tiny cul-de-sac of this name near the famous Café de Flore frequented by the Surrealists so perhaps the title is not a literal indication of the location. The photograph was intended by Lee Miller to be shown in different orientations, both portrait and landscape.

16 **Man Ray**, Paris, France 1931

Man Ray was one of the founders of the New York Dada movement, a surrealist artist and photographer of great significance. He and Lee Miller became lovers and collaborators and he had a formative influence on Lee's photographic practice. Published in TIME magazine April 1932 Article: Rayograms.

17 **Tanja Ramm [with cloak]**, Paris, France 1931 (NC0059-1)

Tanja Ramm, a close friend from Lee Miller's childhood in Poughkeepsie, New York, and in 1929 joined her in Paris. Tanja worked as a model for Mainbocher and other couture houses.

18 **Untitled [Woman with hand on head]**, Paris, France 1931 (NC0098-2)

The soignée hair and manicure reassemble into a troubling image. Is the woman being attacked by a disembodied hand? Or has the whole arrangement morphed into a strange fruit with its stalk and caylx? This and many other interpretations rest with the viewer's choice.

19 **Untitled [Stone]**, Paris, France 1931

The anthropomorphic shape of the rock suggests a pair of breasts. The connection to the severed breast image cannot be established, but the theme may relate to the way Man Ray repeatedly dismembered Lee Miller's body photographically.

20 **Untitled [Window]**, Paris, France c1932 (NC0065)

This early work is an example of Lee Miller's 'Image Trouvé' style. The window featured is remarkably similar to one from her New York studio which was a duplex apartment that she lived and worked from.

21 **Solarised Portrait [thought to be Meret Oppenheim]**, Paris, France 1932 (NC0058-5)

Lee Miller accidentally re-discovered the Sabatier effect where the negative is given a second exposure during development. Man Ray named the technique 'solarisation'. It causes the dark line around the edges of the object and gives the image a dreamlike unreality much admired by the Surrealists.

22 **Fashion study**, Paris, France 1932 (NC0033)

The elegant pose and complicated lighting set up shows Lee learned well from her work modelling for *Vogue* photographers Edward Steichen in the USA and George Hoyningen-Heuné in Paris.

23 **Charlie Chaplin with light fixture**, St Moritz, Switzerland 1932 (NC0203)

The great comic film actor and director Charlie Chaplin was at the climax of his career: His movie City Lights appeared the year after this photograph was taken. Lee Miller met Chaplin in Paris and photographed him then and later in New York.

24 **Self-portrait with headband**, New York Studio, New York, USA c1932 (12-1-C)

This portrait was part of a shoot to show the hair band which was made of a revolutionary new material called plastic for an advertisement. Lee Miller used a half plate studio camera which could not focus at close range, so she would have to shoot a full frame shot making an enlargement to crop for a possible close-up.

25 **Lilian Harvey, solarised portrait**, New York Studio, New York, USA 1933 (NC0050-1)

Although she was British, Lilian Harvey spent most of her childhood and youth in Germany, where she became a star of screen musicals, including the internationally successful Der Kongress tanzt. She later acted in a number of Hollywood movies.

26 **Dorothy Hill**, New York Studio, New York, USA 1933 (NC0031)

Lee Miller made a handful of solarised portraits of her friend Dorothy Hill which are considered society portraits. In early 1933 Lee had a critically acclaimed one-woman show of her photographs at the Julien Levy Gallery in New York – the first and last in her lifetime. *Vanity Fair* listed her among 'the...most distinguished living photographers'.

27 **Scent Bottles**, New York Studio, New York, USA 1933 (NC0035-8)

When Lee Miller returned to New York in 1933 and set up her studio the effects of the Wall Street Crash were still acutely felt. Luckily the Parisian chic of her style impressed art directors who commissioned her work.

28 **Floating Head, Mary Taylor**, New York Studio, New York, USA 1933 (NC0058-8)

Mary Taylor was a young actress on Broadway who came to Lee Miller for photographs for her agent to send to casting directors in Hollywood.

29 **Virgil Thomson, Composer**, New York Studio, New York, USA c1933 (NYS 115-2)

Virgil Thomson wrote the score for the Surrealist opera by Gertrude Stein titled Four Saints in Three Acts, directed by John Houseman. Lee Miller photographed him and the black African-American cast for publicity use.

30 **Joseph Cornell**, New York Studio, New York, USA 1933 (96-2)

This American surrealist artist first exhibited in an exhibition of Surrealism at the Julien Levy Gallery, New York in 1932. In this portrait Lee Miller merges Joseph Cornell's profile with one of his 'objects'. Her photographs of his work from this period constitute an important record as much has been lost.

31 **Aziz Eloui Bey and Lee Miller**, Egypt c1935 (E1119)

Aziz Eloui Bey, Lee Miller's first husband, was well known for his charm and kindness and did everything he could to make her happy. The sheer boredom of the expatriate society soon defeated his efforts. After a period of inactivity Lee began taking pictures by way of escape.

32 **Untitled [Man with basket in doorway]**, Egypt c1936 (E0621)

The doorway is too narrow to admit the man and his basket. The solid impenetrable door is secured with a bar he cannot reach. Perhaps this is Lee Miller's metaphor for the difficulty she found in entering Egyptian society.

33 The Drawbridge of Deir El Soriani Monastery, Wadi Natrun, Egypt c1936 (E0766)

The keep and drawbridge of this desert monastery show how intensely the Coptic monks feared persecution despite the isolation of their abode in Wadi Natrun.

34 Untitled [Stairway], Cairo, Egypt c1936 (E1904)

This image of denied access perhaps reflects Lee Miller's sense of exclusion and lack of engagement with life in Egypt. The visitor can pass on up the stairs but never see in through the barred and draped darkened window.

35 Untitled [Bleached snail shells], Western Desert, Egypt c1936 (E0778)

The snail eggs lie dormant in the sandy bottom of the wadis until the rare event of rain occurs. Then the eggs hatch, the plant seeds germinate and grow in time to provide food for the newly hatched snails before everything is scorched off by the sun and the cycle waits to begin again.

36 Portrait of Space, Al Bulwayeb, Near Siwa, Egypt 1937 (E1905)

An image that suggests longing for escape and freedom, this photograph was published in the London Bulletin. It was the inspiration for the painting titled Le Baiser 1938 by the Belgian Surrealist René Magritte who is thought to have seen a copy in Roland Penrose's home. Published in *London Bulletin*, June 1940.

37 Eileen Agar at the Royal Pavilion, Brighton, England 1937 (A0007)

Eileen Agar was a British surrealist artist and friend of Roland Penrose. She exhibited her work in the first International Surrealist Exhibition in London 1936. The bulge on her abdomen is her Rolleiflex camera. When Picasso saw the photograph he insisted Eileen was pregnant - with a camera. Published in *London Bulletin*, June 1938 in Article: *Shadows and Reliefs*.

38 Brighton Beach, Brighton, East Sussex, England 1937 (A0011)

After enjoying the hot sun and endless fine sand beaches of the Egyptian coast, Lee Miller must have found the shingle beach of Brighton with its well buttoned up holiday makers unusual to point of being exotic.

39 Picnic, Ile Sainte Marguerite, Cannes, France 1937 (P0146)

The party were staying at Hotel Vaste Horizon in Mougins during August and made a day trip to the island. Left to right - Nusch and Paul Éluard, Roland Penrose, Man Ray and his girlfriend Ady Fidelin.

40 Picasso, Hotel Vaste Horizon, Mougins, France 1937 (P0110)

Picasso was among the party of surrealists artists at Hotel Vaste Horizon where Lee Miller and Roland Penrose stayed. He had just finished painting Guernica, and perhaps as an escape from the blackness and horror of that work he painted Lee six times, ebullient and dressed in the costume of a woman from Arles.

41 **Dora Maar,** Mougins, France 1937

Dora Maar (Markovic), a surrealist photographer of great merit, met Lee Miller in Paris where they lived in the same quarter. Lee reproduced this image in her only collage Untitled 1937. These two artists remained friends for the rest of their lives.

42 **From the top of the Great Pyramid,** Giza, Egypt c1937 (E1862)

Lee Miller spurned the usual shots of the Great Pyramid. The shadow stretches over the land and the dwellings of the people in a similar way to the influence of the Pharaohs dominated the land.

43 **The Procession [Bird Tracks in Sand]**, Ain Sukhana, Red Sea, Egypt c1937

The tracks left in the sand give us evidence of the passage of unseen birds and other marine creatures occupying this seemingly deserted beach. The image is typical of Lee Miller's insistence that we should look beyond what is real and readily observable to find unexpected discoveries.

44 **Robin Fedden,** Egypt 1937 (E1139)

A writer and poet, Robin Fedden lectured in English literature at Cairo University. He later worked for the National Trust and wrote on a wide range of subjects. He was an experienced mountaineer and was persuaded to bring his skis for this bizarrely set up photograph.

45 **Untitled [Cotton Sacks]**, Assyut, Egypt 1939 (E1220)

On the cotton farm owned by her friend Gerti Wissa's family in Assyut on the Nile, Lee Miller found these sacks of cotton. She called the place 'The Cloud Factory' imagining it was where clouds were manufactured and stored to await shipping to their destination.

46 **Untitled [Legs: Mafy Miller, unknown, George Hoyningen-Heuné and Roland Penrose]**, Gebel Mawta, Siwa, Egypt 1939 (E1017)

Gebel Mawta is an immense burial ground on the edge of Siwa Oasis, where the ground is honeycombed with tombs. Mafy Miller was Lee Miller's sister in law, and George Hoyningen-Huené was photographing for his famous Egypt book. Roland Penrose, was visiting Lee, under the pretence of being a photographer.

47 **Tea will be a little late today,** London, England 1940 (3850-2)

Lee Miller sought to capture the undoubtedly surreal qualities of the Blitz while portraying the Londoner's in dominatable spirit. Many of her Blitz images were published in the booklet Grim Glory, Pictures of Britain Under Fire, and some were exhibited in the exhibition Britain at War at the Museum of Modern Art, New York in 1941.

48 **St James**, Sussex Gardens, Paddington, London, England 1940 (GG0029)

Work has begun to repair bomb damage inflicted during the blitz. In the face of the continued bombing raids, which could have completely destroyed the church at any time, this represents a testimony of the Londoners' determination.

49 **Dolphin Square**, Sussex Gardens, Paddington, London, England 1940 (GG0015)

The contrast between the gash made by the bomb and bleak formal façade of the remaining building makes the damage seem all the more horrific, especially as it is framed by flimsy net curtains which would not afford any protection.

50 **Eggceptional Achievement**, London, England 1940 (GG0033)

The grounded barrage balloon, thought to be on Hampstead Heath, was published in 'Grim Glory - Pictures of Britain Under Fire' 1941 captioned as: 'The geese that laid a silver egg'. Lee Miller's own title for the image was Eggceptional Achievement.

51 **Revenge on Culture**, London, England 1940 (GG0040)

The woman's medieval shield was not an effective defence against the bombs of the Luftwaffe. Seen through Lee Miller's camera as she lies among the rubble she becomes a metaphor for the destruction of beauty and culture. Published in 'Grim Glory - Pictures of Britain Under fire' 1941 and also in Arabic Listener, Books and Culture supplement Feb 1942.

52 **Remington Silent**, London, England 1940 (GG0041)

The old saying 'A picture is worth a thousand words' resonates in this image through the agency of which The Remington Silent typewriter regains its ability to communicate the agony of the Blitz. Published in 'Grim Glory-Pictures of Britain Under Fire' 1941.

53 **Shattered Roof of University College**, London, England 1940 (GG0039)

Although mainly intact, the fragile roof of the college was easily pierced by shrapnel and bomb fragments, allowing rain water in to form a puddle that reflects the neoclassical dome high above. Published in Grim Glory - Pictures of Britain Under Fire' 1941.

54 **Fire Masks**, Downshire Hill, London, England 1941 (3840-8)

When the German bombing cut off the electricity to the *Vogue* studio, Lee Miller used exterior locations for her fashion shots. The eye-shields worn by these women were issued to Air Raid Protection wardens (Roland Penrose was one) to protect them from incendiary bombs. One holds an air-raid warden's whistle. The woman on the right is *Vogue* fashion editor Isabel Tisdall (née Gallegos)

The location is the entrance to the air raid shelter in garden of Roland's house in Hampstead. Published in *American Vogue*, July 1941, page 60 Article: British Woman Under Fire.

55 **Good and bad posture**, *Vogue Studio*, London, England 1942

The glass orbs are lamps from the studio lighting rig, and the two figures were photographed separately and pasted into the layout before the images was re-photographed. The finesse of this work demonstrates the close co-operation between Lee Miller and the art director, Alex Kroll. Published in *British Vogue*, February 1942.

56 **Roland Penrose with mumps**, Downshire Hill, London, England 1942 (4694-5)

Lee Miller seldom photographed the people she was closest to, so it is somewhat ironic that one of the few pictures of Roland Penrose that exists is this mocking study of him suffering with mumps.

57 **Lee Miller, *Vogue Studio***, London, England 1943 (NC0001-1)

David E. Scherman encouraged Lee Miller to become a US Army war correspondent for *Vogue* magazine. This accreditation gave her access to places and stories denied to civilian journalists and after D Day allowed her to cover the Allies advance in Europe.

58 **David E. Scherman, dressed for war**, London, England 1943 (NC0051-11)

David E. Scherman, seen here suitably dressed for war, was a distinguished photo-journalist for LIFE Magazine who worked closely with Lee Miller from 1942 to 1945. They made a highly effective team covering the US Forces in Europe after D Day including the Russian – American link at Torgau, the liberation of Dachau, and the fall of Munich.

59 **Henry Moore taken during the filming of 'Out of Chaos'**, Holborn Underground, London, England 1943 (5282-20)

The sculptor Henry Moore, working as a war artist, was making sketches of people sheltering from the air raids for his famous "Sleepers" series. On this occasion he was being filmed for a documentary titled 'Out of Chaos' by Two Cities Films, directed by Jill Craigie.

60 **US Army nurses' billet**, Churchill Hospital, Oxford, England 1943 (4834-122)

Taken as part of the shoot for Lee Miller's short article on 'American Army Nurses'. Lee wrote about the nurses: 'the Presbyterian Hospital of New York has taken over the Churchill Hospital in Oxford .... (The Nurses) went quietly about their business of healing and caring for the American Armed forces.' Published in *British Vogue* in May 1943.

61 **Bad Burns Case**, 44th Evacuation Hospital, Bricqueville, Normandy, France 1944 (5848a-56)

Lee Miller wrote; 'A bad burns case asked me to take his picture as he wanted to see how funny he looked. It was pretty grim and I didn't focus good.'

62 **Surgeon and anaesthetist at 44th Evacuation Hospital,** Bricqueville, Normandy, France 1944 (5848-64)

The quiet concentration of the surgical team belies the fact that they could hear the battle for St Lô raging only a few miles away. This was Lee Miller's first assignment as a photojournalist, and it established her domination of *Vogue* features for the next eighteen months.

63 **For cycling:** white rayon smocked with blue; apron-overskirt nearly meets behind,Eiffel Tower, Paris, France 1944 (5929-74)

Lee Miller's description reads; 'For cycling: white rayon smocked dress with blue; apron-overskirt nearly meets behind'. The extravagant use of fabric was an act of resistance, denying resources to the enemy and defying the edicts to save material. Published in *British Vogue*, October 1944.

64 **Rose Descat's dark red felt hat** rises high, fits closely - a line Paris loves. The waterfall of scarf is electric blue silk jersey, Paris, France 1944 (5940-117)

Lee Miller wrote; 'Rose Descat's dark red felt hat rises high, fits closely - a line Paris loves. The waterfall of scarf is electric blue silk jersey'. The empty hat stands hint at the acute shortage of material at that time. Published in *British Vogue*, November 1944.

65 **The veiled Eiffel Tower from the Palais de Chaillot, [Paris under Snow]** Paris, France 1944 (6164-155)

Captioned as: PARIS UNDER SNOW, Lee Miller wrote: 'It brought fun to the boys and girls, snowballing; brought hardships, too...veiled the Eiffel Tower, and outlined figures, animate and inanimate, with the precision of a Chinese painting.' Published in *British Vogue*, March 1945.

66 **Snow capped statue**, Jardins des Tuileries, Paris, France 1944 (6164-102)

The years Lee Miller endured the heat of Egypt may have given her a sense of irony when she photographed this Pharaonic style sculpture in her image during the harsh winter of 1944-45. Published *British Vogue*, March 1945.

67 **Picasso and Lee Miller in his studio**, Liberation of Paris, Rue des Grands-Augustins, Paris, Brittany, France 1944 (NC0002-1)

Lee Miller went to find Picasso in the artist's studio during the liberation of Paris. Picasso embraced Lee with effusive warmth, declaring: 'This is marvellous, the first Allied soldier I should see is a woman, and she is you!'

68 **Colette**, France's Greatest Living Woman Writer', 9 rue de Beaujolais, Paris, France 1944 (6064-103)

Sidonie-Gabrielle Colette, France's greatest woman writer, aged 71, continued to work in her apartment in the Palais Royal although she was mostly confined to bed. During the occupation she had written Journal à rebours (1941) and De ma fenêtre (1942) Her most famous work, GiGi, would be published later in 1944.

69 **Jean Cocteau at home**, Paris, France 1944 (5940-41)

Lee Miller arrived in Paris 27th August 1944 missing the liberation of Paris by two days because she had been under arrest following her coverage of the Siege of St Malo. She found Jean Cocteau in his apartment in the Palais Royal. Lee had starred in Cocteau's film The Blood of a Poet in 1930. She wrote; 'We fell into each other's arms. He's looking incredibly well and younger than I thought possible ...' Published in *British Vogue*, October 1944.

70 **Lee Miller at entrance to St Malo Fortress**, St Malo, France 1944 (NC0178-12)

David E. Scherman arrived at the moment the Allies captured the Cité d'Aleth which dominates the port. Lee Miller had covered the four day battle close to the fighting, witnessing severe casualties among the G.I.'s, some of whom had become her buddies.

71 **Fall of the Citadel, Aerial bombardment**, St Malo, France 1944 (5918-55R6)

The aerial bombardment of the citadel using high explosives did little damage to the German positions tunnelled into the rock, and the subsequent assault by US soldiers was repelled with heavy losses.

The Rolleiflex Lee Miller used did not have a telephoto lens, so the explosion is as close as it looks in the picture – being only 700 yards away.

72 **Paul Delvaux and René Magritte**, Brussels, Belgium 1944 (6104-160)

In November 1944 Lee Miller was in liberated Brussels, where, she wrote recording René Magritte's dramatic change of style. *'He has abandoned the dry, stilted manner like village posters and paints now like streaky Renoir and has a passion for varicoloured naked ladies and mystic bouquets.'* Published in *American Vogue*, March 1945.

73 **Copains discussing the war**, Alsace, France 1945 (6185-88)

As they pushed the German army back towards the Rhine the Allies were joined by many French and other nationalities for some of the bitterest fighting that took place in Europe.

74 **Burning surface coal mines**, Duren, Germany 1945 (1-319-R5B)

The locomotive and the eerie stillness of this desolate landscape in this image gives us a reference to the surrealist painter Giorgio de Chirico. Lee Miller's surrealist eye was always present, even in the grimmest circumstances.

75 **Last Leap - The Rhine, Kingelputz prison**, Cologne, Germany 1945 (6268-3)

In this prison the Gestapo held up to 700 prisoners who were systematically tortured and often executed. Lee Miller arrived on the day of its liberation, photographing the freed prisoners, some of whom had been scheduled for execution that day. She described this woman as a 'Displaced person - patient and exhausted'. Published in *British Vogue*, May 1945.

76 **Cologne Cathedral**, Cologne, Germany 1945 (6268-55)

Cologne was heavily bombed and fiercely held by the Germans against the US advance until it fell on 5th March. The cathedral, which dates from the 13th Century, took many direct hits. The rubble at the foot of the gothic columns gives an impression of fallen leaves in a forest. Published in *British Vogue*, May 1945.

77 **Steel spiderweb - Roof of The Festhalle**, Frankfurt, Germany 1945 (21-14)

The structural steel of the dome of The Festhalle, Frankfurt is reduced to a spider's web. This destruction of emblematic city buildings on a massive scale seemed a just desert to Lee Miller following her own experiences in the Blitz. Published in *British Vogue*, June 1945.

78 **Inside a great chemical plant**, Ludwigshaven, Germany 1945 (19-56)

Lee Miller wrote 'Ludwigshaven is a mess. It's a worthy mess however. ... (it) had been one of the greatest chemical plants in the world before the air force adopted it as a target. ... Now it was tangled and razed and beaten up and would never deliver the nitric acid which is in the tank cars, tossed crazily around and leaking vapour and dripping poison.'

79 **Captured German guards** who had donned civilian clothes in the hope of escaping, Buchenwald, Germany 1945 (54-20)

The guards had donned civilian clothes in the hope of escaping. Lee Miller's caption reads; Punishment: S.S. Guards who tortured prisoners, beg mercy on their knees, are beaten by ex-prisoners. Published in *American Vogue*, June 1945 and in *British Vogue*, June 1945.

80 **Orderly furnaces of the crematorium**, Buchenwald, Germany 1945 (51-28)

Appalled by the vast scale of the industrialised murder in the concentration camps, Lee Miller's caption contains biting sarcasm and reads; 'Orderly furnaces to burn bodies' Published in *American Vogue*, June 1945.

81 **Detail of released prisoners in striped prison dress...**, Buchenwald, Germany 1945 (51-25)

This is the cropping used by *Vogue* and it spares us from seeing the faces of the prisoners as they contemplate the remains of their fellow men. The size of the pile and the casual way they have been dumped continues the dialogue. Published in *American Vogue*, June 1945.

82 **Horrors of a concentration camp**, unforgettable, unforgivable, Buchenwald, Germany 1945 (51-20)

The camp crematorium had run out of fuel some days earlier, so there was no concealing the large number of prisoners who died of hunger, disease and other forms of murder. Lee Miller stated the horrors she witnessed were 'unforgettable (and) unforgivable'.

83 **Suicided Volkssturm Commander; Walter Doenicke**, Town Hall, Leipzig, Germany 1945 (58-54)

A man in the uniform of a Volkssturm (Home Guard) Commander lies dead on the floor of the town hall office next to the office filled by the suicided family of the city treasurer Kurt Lisso. Lee Miller's photograph notes that the scales of justice held by the statue outside the window now hang level.

84 **Dead SS prison guard floating in canal**, Dachau, Germany 1945 (76-91)

Lee Miller wrote: 'The small canal bounding the camp was a floating mess of SS in their spotted camouflage suits and studded boots. They slithered along on the current with a dead dog or two and smashed rifles.' The image contains an unexpected spiritual comment as the man appears to leave the earth and journey towards the light.

85 **Dead deportees lie beside the rail track**, Dachau, Germany 1945 (76-22)

Lee Miller wrote: 'The railway siding into the camp runs past quite a few swell villas and the last train of dead and semi dead deportees was long enough to extend past them.' The train had left Buchenwald thirty days earlier carrying 3102 prisoners. The G.I.'s found only one survivor.

86 **Freed prisoners scavenging in the rubbish dump**, Dachau Concentration Camp, Germany 1945 (76-49)

Lee Miller wrote: 'Prisoners were prowling these heaps, some of which were burning in the hope of finding something more presentable than what they were wearing already'.

87 **Lee Miller in Hitler's bathtub**, Hitler's apartment, Prinzregentenplatz 16, Munich, Germany 1945 (79-19R6)

A tip off from the signal corps got Lee Miller and David E. Scherman access to Hitler's house which only a few hours earlier had been taken over by the US Army as a communications post. Lee wrote "The house was in perfect condition, including electricity and hot water and heat available and electric refrigerator. (Electricity and water is on all over the town)."

88 **Hitler's house [Berghof] on fire** set by SS Troops', Obersalzberg, Bavaria, Germany 1945 (80-45)

Lee Miller and David E. Scherman witnessed what Scherman described as 'The funeral pyre of the Third Reich' Hitler's house 'Wachenfeld' was in flames after the retreating SS had torched it. The war ended two days later.

89 **Statues covered by camouflage nets, Schloss Klessheim,** Salzburg, Austria 1945 (81-16)

Lee Miller wrote; '... a fantastically camouflaged palace which once belonged to Archduke [Ludwig Viktor of Austria] and recently had been Hitler's summer headquarters became the Third Division HQ'. The spectacle of the attempted concealment of the statuary with camouflage nets may have reminded Lee of a landscapes by the surrealist artist Yves Tanguy.

90 **Nearly all these children will die** in next few years if not now, Wilhelminen hospital, Vienna, Austria 1945 (336-48)

In Vienna gangsters had stolen all the hospital drugs, as later portrayed in the movie The Third Man. Lee Miller wrote; 'Pics of starved children in Wilhelmina Hospital where nuns work...nearly all these children will die in next few years if not now'.

91 **Laszlo Bardossy, fascist ex-Prime Minister of Hungary, facing the firing squad**, Budapest, Hungary 1946 (529-M46-16)

Lee Miller wrote: 'I was hanging out of a window when war criminal Lazlo Bardossy, ex-prime minister of Hungary and declarer of war on America, was executed...Bardossy's voice orated in a high-pitched rasp "God save Hungary from all these bandits".'

92 **'The eyes of Sibiu'**, Piata Mica, Sibiu, Romania 1946 (529-M54-50)

Lee Miller wrote, 'I remembered Sibiu as a mysterious looking town. There are staircases in the streets, arcades under buildings, and the slanting roofs had little windows let into them, the shape of peering, prying, calculating eyes.'

93 **Max Ernst and Dorothea Tanning**, Oak Creek Canyon, Sedona, Arizona, USA 1946 (A0227)

In 1946 *American Vogue* invited Lee Miller and Roland Penrose to New York. After the public relations commitments were over they went to find their old friends, the surrealist artists Max Ernst and Dorothea Tanning. The way Dorothy rails at Max in this picture suggests Lee was aware of the creative tension between the two in a male dominated arena, something she was familiar with from her life with Man Ray and that which would repeat with Roland Penrose.

94 **Roland Penrose with Man Ray**, Vine street, Los Angeles, USA 1946 (12766Q-340)

Man Ray fled Paris in 1940 ahead of the German occupation and settled in Hollywood where he had a studio apartment on Vine Street. Lee Miller uses the mirror to give us both profile and full-face in the same portrait of the two longest loves of her life.

95 **Hampstead Fair**, Hampstead, London, England 1949 (NC0163)

After years of black-out and austerity during the war, the return of the fair to London with its blaze of light, colour, music and frivolity is celebrated here with this multiple exposure.

96 **Saul Steinberg** adding the finishing touches to the Long Man of Wilmington, East Sussex, England 1952 (FF0280)

Saul Steinberg the American cartoonist was staying with Lee Miller and Roland Penrose at Farleys on the occasion of his exhibition at the ICA (Institute of Contemporary Art) in London. They visited the Neolithic figure of The Long Man of Wilmington on the nearby South Downs, and Saul, the master of line drawing, pretended to add the finishing touches.

97 **Picasso embracing his sculpture** Femme à la poussette, Vallauris, France 1954 (P1040)

Picasso embraces the baby made of potshards from his sculpture Femme à la poussette. Roland Penrose was just beginning to write his biography of Picasso and he and Lee Miller made many visits to Picasso's homes. Lee photographed Picasso and his lifestyle more than 1,000 times.

98 **Georges Limbour and Jean Dubuffet**, Farleys House, East Sussex, England 1955 (FF0706)

Georges Limbour, the poet and Jean Dubuffet the painter visited Farleys House. Dubuffet was in England for his first exhibition at the ICA in London. Lee Miller's reflection in the glass is also caught in the photograph.

99 **Miró at the zoo [Hornbill]**, London Zoo, London, England 1964 (A0116)

Joan Miró, the Catalan painter, visited England on the occasion of a major retrospective exhibition of his work at the Tate Gallery London. Desmond Morris, who was then the director of London Zoo took Miró on a private tour, and arranged for him to handle some of the animals.

100 **Lee Miller the hostess takes it easy**, Farleys House, Muddles Green, Sussex, England 1953 (LM131-5)

Man Ray once said Lee Miller could make more work for other people than anyone else he knew. Roland Penrose's image appeared in Lee's article for *British Vogue* titled Working Guests published July 1953. It implied that while everyone else was busy renovating the old farm house Lee was taking a nap.

SELECT BIBLIOGRAPHY

Bouhassane, Ami. *Lee Miller, a Life with Food, Friends and Recipes*. Farleys House and Gallery 2017

Roberts, Hilary. *Lee Miller, a Woman's War*. Thames & Hudson 2015

Haworth-Booth, Mark. *The Art of Lee Miller*. V&A publications 2007

Penrose, Antony, editor, with foreword by David E. Scherman. *Lee Miller's War*. Thames & Hudson 2007

Calvocoressi, Richard. *Lee Miller. Portraits from a Life*. Thames & Hudson 2002

Calvocoressi Richard, Keith Hartley, Antony Penrose et all. *The Surrealist and The Photographer*. National Galleries of Scotland 2001

Livingstone, Jane. *Lee Miller Photographer*. California International Arts Foundation 1992

Man Ray. *Self Portrait*. Andre Deutsch 1963

Penrose, Antony. *The Lives of Lee Miller*. Thames & Hudson 1984

Penrose, Antony. *Lee Miller's War*. Foreword by David E. Scherman. Thames & Hudson 2014

Penrose, Roland. *Scrap Book*. Thames & Hudson 1981

Penrose, Roland. *Man Ray*. Thames & Hudson 1975

TECHNICAL NOTE BY ANTONY PENROSE

Lee Miller's preferred camera was a Rolleiflex which she used for nearly all her work apart from when she was in her own studio or the *Vogue* studio when she used a half-plate life camera. Shortly after D-Day she looted a 35mm Zeiss Contax which she carried for the next 18 months on her travels but she retained the Rolleiflex as her main camera. This was fortunate for the Lee Miller Archives because the 50mm square negatives from the Rolleiflex are easier to conserve and print from than 35mm.

Lee Miller mainly used Kodak plate and roll film but when in Europe during the World War II she used anything she could lay her hands on. Most of her printing was done on Kodak paper. During the war shortage of materials meant the lab printed on whatever was available and the Lee Miller Archives has some strange sizes and qualities of print dating from this period.

ACKNOWLEDGEMENTS

Lee Miller Gelatin Silver Prints printed by Carole Callow at the Lee Miller Archives

Digital imaging by Lance Downie at the Lee Miller Archives

Exhibition tour organised by Ami Bouhassane and Tracy Leeming

Rights management by Kerry Negahban and Lori Inglis Hall

Translated to Italian by Alessandra Chiappini

FARLEY FARM HOUSE TOURS

For more information regarding visiting Farleys House, the home of Lee Miller, please got to **www.farleyshouseandgallery.co.uk**

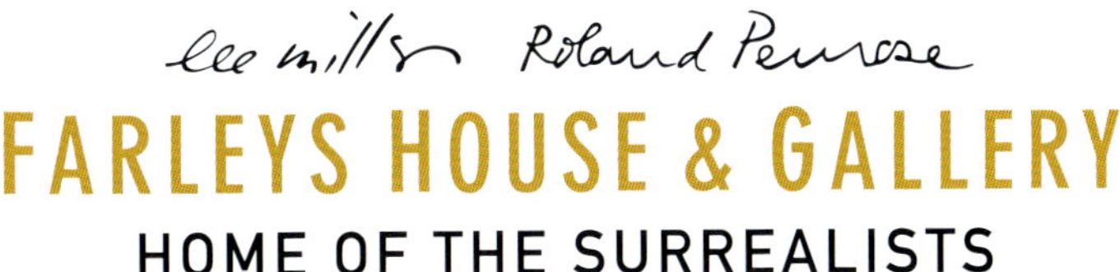